67 WAYS TO AMUSE YOURSELF

(in 2 Minutes or Less)

by

Dick Wolfsie

Life Press
9850 E. 30th Street
Indianapolis, IN 46229
(317) 365-5911 • fax (317) 396-5904
e-mail: lifepress@lifepress.net

Cover designed by David Finley, Indianapolis, IN
Book production by LifePress, Indianapolis, IN
Printed in the USA

10 9 8 7 6 5 4 3 2 1
First edition

In Memory of Art Buchwald

Mr. Buchwald, you were an inspiriation to me for 40 years. Thanks for all the laughter you brought into the world.

PREFACE

The short humorous essay has a long tradition in American literature. As far back as the Pilgrims...like anyone cares...

Here are 69 of my favorite humor columns, all written over the past three years and published weekly in Indiana newspapers. I know the cover says 67, but I counted wrong and it was too late to change the title. I am funny, but I can't add. Neither can the people who administer the SATs (#52) so I don't feel so bad. Or is it badly. My proofreader, Heidi, would know (#36).

Thinking of something funny every week is not easy (#43).

Humor is very personal. You may get hysterical when you read # 45 and be bored to death by #78. But here's the good news. You've only wasted two minutes of your valuable time. You can't say that when you've just walked out of a lousy $8.50 movie.

Of course, the nice thing about reading columns in a newspaper is that when you really love one, you can cut it out and stick it on the fridge; and if you really hate one, you can stick it in the garbage.

But don't throw this book away. Remember, you can always re-gift it.

By the way, many people have asked me if the columns are arranged in any particular order. Okay, I'll explain this again. They go from number 1 to number 69.

So sit back in your easy chair. Or lie down on the couch. Or adjust your car seat. Or get into bed. Or get on your exercise bike. Have a few laughs, two minutes at a time.

TABLE OF CONTENTS

LIGHT OF MY LIFE

It was very early on a Sunday morning. I had just parked next to Martinsville High School where I was giving a speech. I jumped out of my car, slammed the door, and stood there in total darkness gaping at my SUV.

"Whattaya doing, Dick Wolfsie?" came a voice from behind me. "Why are you staring at your car?"

It was a woman about to go inside to hear my presentation in the school cafeteria.

"I'm waiting to be sure my dome light goes out," I said.

At the time, it seemed like a reasonable response. And a pretty sensible thing to do. But the more I thought about it, the more concerned I became about my behavior.

I realized that I've lacked confidence in the dome light of all my cars since the Reagan Administration. I feel bad about this because I am sure that millions of dollars of research went into this technology. Many questions needed to be answered before they could add this accessory.

How quickly should the light go out?

Should it fade out or just blink off?

Should it work 24/7?

It was that last one that made me start to obsess. I realized that the light also stays on for 30 seconds during the day, but I had never noticed it, so for the last week I've been squinting my eyes like crazy because there's no way I'm walking away from that car if there's one chance in a million that light is going to be on all day.

What's really sad is that I should be taking advantage of this technology for its time-saving and safety aspects instead of squandering my life waiting for my dome light to go out.

Here's how I figured it: once a night (30 seconds) for 20 years. That's 219,000 seconds or six hours of my life wasted. (This easily trumps sitting through a class in Early Puritan Literature or two hours in traffic class for a speeding ticket.)

Now I'm starting to lament all that lost time waiting for that infernal light to go out. Those six hours could have been used for important things like:

- Waiting around to see if my alarm clock will still go off if I've awakened early

- Balancing my checkbook with pencil and paper to be sure my calculator is not broken

- Standing in front of my microwave for three minutes to be sure the timer works

- Backing up my TiVo with my VHS recorder, which is kind of ironic because I still don't really trust that machine either. Never have.

The bottom line, I guess, is that I have never been fully comfortable with technology. In my heart, I believe that several phone calls from NBC asking me to guest host the *Tonight Show* were inadvertently deleted from my answering machine, and I'd bet my iPod (if I had one) that somewhere in cyberspace there is an e-mail asking me to take over for Andy Rooney when he moves into the retirement home for curmudgeons.

I know that while some of you think I am very odd, others are nodding their heads because they have the very same lack of confidence in their dome lights.

Oh, and one final thing. I'm a little tired of telling people that their car headlights are still on when they walk away from the car, only to have them say in the most sarcastic tone:

"This is a new car, they go out automatically."

Yeah, right.

COUCH TOMATO

My wife is home convalescing and has to spend a week downstairs on the living room couch. This gives me the opportunity to show her how much I love her and how much she can depend on me.

After all, that's what husbands are for.

So, because I am a good husband, I'm not leaving the house even for a second, just in case my wife needs anything. Uh, could you excuse me for a second? She's calling me. "Yes, of course, sweetheart, I'll get you a glass of water, that's what I'm here for…there you go."

So, as I was about to say, my wife is a very good patient and I'm sure that…"What's that dear? Yes, I got the water from the tap. Oh, you wanted bottled water? Of course, that would be my pleasure. Funny, you usually say bottled water is a waste of money. Let me just run to the store. Your wish is my command."

Sorry for the interruption. Anyway, as I was saying, I think it's important that a husband show his love in any small way possible..."What's that, sweetheart? You want some tomato soup? Of course, whatever your heart desires. There you go. Hot and delicious."

Now back to my point about a husband's commitment. Hold on, excuse me a sec, my wife is calling. "Yes, dear, that was creamy tomato soup. No, I didn't know you liked regular tomato soup better. Sure, I'll get the regular tomato soup next time I'm at the store....You mean right now? Okay, even though it's 90 degrees outside, I'd be happy to just jump into the car and go to the store."

"Here's the soup dear....Oh, and I got you *Pride and Prejudice* from the video store as you requested. Here it is. Enjoy."

So, as I was saying. A good marriage is... "What's that dear? You wanted it on DVD, not VHS, so you could see the outtakes? But you've never wanted to see outtakes before. I see. You have never had to lie on a couch all day with nothing to do, either. Okay, no problem. I'll be right back. I left the car running, anyway."

I'm back. Now, for you husbands reading this, try to take a lesson from me on how important it is to be a loving caretaker... "What's that, Mary Ellen? You want another pillow? Sure, hold on I'll get you one...Here you go. Yes, it's a down pillow.

All our pillows are down pillows. For 25 years all our pillows have been down pillows. But you feel like a foam rubber pillow? Well, not a problem. Let me just go down in the basement and look through 25 years of stuff and find that one foam rubber pillow we never used because, IF YOU REMEMBER, YOU HATE FOAM RUBBER PILLOWS. Here you go. I hope this makes you happy."

I'm sorry for all these interruptions. But it's very important to be a supportive spouse when… "What's that, Mary Ellen? No, I didn't realize that the bulb on our cathedral ceiling was out. Actually, I didn't even know we had bulbs up there, but then I'm not lying on my back with absolutely nothing to do all day but think of things…sorry, let me get a new bulb and see if I can find someone in the neighborhood with a 40-foot ladder."

So, just to wrap things up before I go out to the store for the third time today—to get my wife a copy of *People Magazine*, which she never reads because she has always said that it is a stupid waste of time—I hope that if your wife ever has to spend an entire week on the couch, you'll be as good natured about it as I am.

After all, that's what husbands are for.

LIVING THE
SHINGLE LIFE

As a result of hail damage, the Wolfsies got a new roof, courtesy of our insurance company. I have never been up on my roof, so I had no idea what was going on up there.

I know it's a cliché, but the Wolfsies are just happy to have a roof over our heads.

Which is also a pretty concise summary of what I know about roofs.

Or is it rooves?

My wife and I were sitting in our living room while the workmen banged, hammered, and stapled the new shingles into place. I am no handyman, but I did know that overseeing the project was probably important in assessing their workmanship. I decided to impress Mary Ellen with my interest in the project.

"Mary Ellen, they sure sound like they know what they're doing, don't they? I mean that rat-a-tat, that clatter, is clearly the work of experienced craftsmen."

"I sure hope you're right, Dick," she said. "We really have no idea what they are doing up there. Maybe they're installing the flashing or shingles improperly. Or using the wrong type of nails."

I had never thought of that.

I *do* worry that my dentist will pull the wrong tooth or that my orthopedist will operate on the wrong knee.

If now I started to worry about my shingles, I would have to be heavily sedated most of the day. But Mary Ellen felt I should be more knowledgeable about what was happening to our roof.

I finally decided to confess my ignorance.

"Look, Mary Ellen, I wouldn't know a shingle that was improperly installed if one hit me in the head."

"Seems to me you'd be missing a pretty good clue, right there, Dick. Look, we can't just sit here while nine people crawl all over our roof. I feel like we should be more involved—like Lowell."

At this point, I should mention my friend Lowell lives next door. He was also getting a new roof.

But Lowell is an activist homeowner.

I know this because while we were having this shingles conversation, Lowell was scampering across his own roof inspecting the work site.

Occasionally he would say something to the contractor on the roof and the guy would nod his head. If Lowell hadn't been in his pajamas he would have appeared to be even more in charge.

After I saw this, I decided to give Lowell a call.

"Hi, Lowell. It's Dick. Say, I saw you up on your roof. How's everything going up there?"

"Just fine. The job was done well. I chose a wind-resistant, high-grade fiberglass product. I wanted to watch them to make sure the multidimensional shingles were properly alternated.

Also, I checked the flashing and made sure the vents were installed so that the attic could properly breathe … Dick, Dick are you there?"

"Yada, yada, yada … Look, all this roof stuff is really over my head. Do me a favor, the next time you're on your roof, could you kind of saunter over toward my roof and give it a quick look-see?"

Lowell declined the offer. He said that my roof was not his concern and that I needed to accept responsibility for my own home repairs.

He said that learning how to find my balance while negotiating the pitch of the roof would test my resolve and strength.

Sorry, Lowell. I'm not going to fall for that.

4

IT'S NOT EASY BEING GREEN

When our son started college, we had the normal parental concerns. Was he eating right? Did he have his class schedule in order? In addition, all parents wonder how their young adults will handle the temptations of new-found freedoms.

We were both anxious when we joined our son at a local fast-food restaurant for lunch. With all our fears, some justified, some not, there was one thing we could never have anticipated. Brett had turned green.

I wish I were making this up, but while Mary Ellen and I sat across from Brett as he devoured the KFC chicken fingers, we noticed that his skin had a grayish-green tint to it. At first, we were alarmed. We had sent Brett to college with the hopes of a good education. We hoped that something would set in.

We hadn't expected gangrene.

"Brett, have you noticed that you are turning green?" I asked nonchalantly, trying to hide my concern.

My wife, never wanting to seem negative, interrupted my query. "It's a lovely shade of green, of course. But you weren't that color when you left home."

Brett seemed unnerved by the observation. He looked at his arms and his hands. Then he tightened his face, gritted his teeth, and growled, "Don't make me angry. You wouldn't like me when I'm angry."

The idea that my son might really be The Hulk was a bit disconcerting, but parents are often surprised to find out their teens' secret lives.

Brett explained that he had noticed the change in hue after showering and drying off with the towels we had bought him for his dorm room. This brought a glare from my wife who had wanted to splurge on plushier accessories but had been convinced otherwise by her cheap husband who thought if Amazon.com was good enough for books, it was good enough for towels.

Now that the source of the discoloration had been identified, Mary Ellen went into a spasm of laughter, mostly out of relief that Brett did not have a rare tropical disease. Knowing this would end up as a newspaper column, I tried out all my jokes

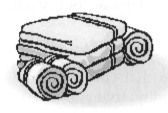

on Brett, like, "You should start a garden, now that you have a green thumb." Then I went into a musical rendition of "It's Not Easy Being Green," using my very best Kermit the Frog impersonation. Mary Ellen, at this point, would have laughed at anything, thankful we didn't need to make an appointment at the Mayo Clinic.

It was time to go back to the dorm. I helped carry some of the items from the car to Brett's room. Brett's roommate, Connor, was there practicing his guitar. "Hey, Connor, did you notice that Brett has turned green?" I blurted out, still a bit giddy with the potential for more green jokes.

"That's really odd," said Connor, looking at his arm. "I noticed that I was turning kind of blue."

Sure enough, Connor's arms had an attractive sky-blue tint, which my wife and I immediately noticed matched his towels over on the shelf. Amazon.com sure knows how to sell towels.

One of the fears that Mary Ellen and I always had was that Brett and his roommate would clash, but this was not what we had anticipated. I gave Brett some cash to buy new towels. I told him to go to Kmart and pick out something he liked.

We see Brett on occasional weekends. It's always fun to see what color he is.

5

END OF STORY

I recently spent a few days at the 2006 Indianapolis Gift and Hobby Show hawking (I mean, selling) my books.

The coolest part of the event was having people come by and talk to me about having seen some of the quirky entries in my brand new, revised book *Indiana Curiosities,* such as the man with the 500-pound orchid or the pneumatic pumpkin launcher. I related stories of the many oddities and wonders I discovered here in the Hoosier state. People seemed captivated as I recounted my adventures.

Then I went home.

My wife used to hang on my every word. Recently, however, she has become a bit complacent with my storytelling after hearing me rant for 25 years.

I told Mary Ellen that a man at the show had purchased two boxes of my books. He wanted to take them on a business trip to Asia as gifts for his overseas associates to reveal the wonderful curiosities of his home state.

"Mary Ellen, I must tell you this. I was selling my books at the Gift and Hobby Show when this man walked up to me and…"

"Where was his wife?"

"What do you mean, where was his wife?"

"Isn't it mostly women who shop at that show? Did he leave his wife at home?"

"Look, this has nothing to do with the story. So, anyway, this guy…"

"Maybe he was divorced. How old was he? I have some single friends at work who…"

"Look, here's the point of the story. He came over to me and set down the stuff he had purchased, and…"

"Oh, what did he buy? Was it one of those cloths that absorbs spills? Those are great. You bought one two years ago. Did you get any of those while you were at the show?"

"Could we get back to the story? The man mentioned to me that he travels the world on business and…"

"Well, no wonder he doesn't have a wife. How can you expect to have a permanent relationship when you are running off to all four corners of the earth…"

"Mary Ellen, please. Here's the great part of the story. The guy has a business in Singapore and..."

"Singapore! That would be a great place to visit some day. Did he recommend any hotels? Oh, this is very exciting. Can we pick up some brochures at the travel agent this week?"

"Look, let me try this one more time. The guy comes up to me and says he wants to buy my books and..."

"Well, why didn't you sell him a couple of boxes of books to take to Singapore? That way, the people over there would get a better idea of the wonderful oddities we have here in Indiana. I can't believe you didn't think of that."

"That's exactly what I did."

"Well, what took you so long to get to the point. You used to be such a good storyteller."

6

SPACE CADET

I believe that when God makes a human being he has a little fairness checklist. "Okay, this child will have a great nose, but his ears will stick out (that's me, by the way). Or, "I'll make this baby become a great hockey player someday, but I'll give him the worst case of psoriasis in North America." Or, "I'll make this girl a real looker, but she'll be a little shy of an Irish Setter when it comes to brains."

I know a lot of you feel your children are perfect. Trust me, you are not being objective. Okay, your kid has a 3.8 average in school; she is getting a volleyball scholarship to Notre Dame and is drop-dead gorgeous. Fine. But have you heard her sing? Can she cook? And what a temper!

When the good Lord made me, for example, he gave me lots of creativity but there was just no room left for an attention span. I mention all this because I am trying to justify my most recent adventure into space where my wife just shook her head, incredulous that I ever get through the day. And there are lots of examples.

Recently, I lost my appointment book. I found it a week later in the freezer. (I had placed it there while trying to extract a quart of Cherry Garcia with my two hands, then left the book behind the frozen meatballs and Eskimo Pies.)

One time my mother-in-law called and asked if I'd take her Impala into the shop because of a Chevy recall. I headed over to her house, picked up the keys at the front door, and drove over to the dealership...

"Hello, I'm here because of the Chevy Impala recall," I said to the service clerk.

"Well, that's fine, Dick, but you're driving a Jeep Cherokee."

"I was just checking to make sure you were still in business. I'll be back soon."

There was the time I lost my cell phone for a week. Then one afternoon I walked past the dog food container in the garage and the Iams MiniChunks were playing "The Star-Spangled Banner." This not only intrigued me, but it put the dog in a patriotic lather, as well. I wrote Iams a letter with a suggestion to make their food play music that shows loyalty (dogs love that stuff), but I got no response. You're probably wondering how the phone got in the dog food. There is a logical explanation. I don't have a clue what it could be, but there has to be one.

Here's the latest. Last week my family returned home from a trip to Germany. I had left my car in the TV station parking lot, but when my wife dropped me off at the station Sunday night, the car was gone. Missing! Stolen! Panicked, I called the station manager, business manager, and chief engineer. All were perplexed.

"Who would steal a car from a parking lot that is monitored all day? And, no offense, Dick, but who would steal a 1992 Taurus?"

Good point. But it was gone. The station security people spent several hours looking at surveillance tapes the next day, but their search was in vain. I called the police. Nothing had been found.

My wife was not very sympathetic. "Are you sure you left it at the station?"

"Of course, I am sure. What kind of a space cadet do you think I am?"

This was a risky remark. Apparently, in her free time Mary Ellen has actually made a list of words to describe my lack of focus. No, you will not see the list.

The next day I went to the post office to pick up our vacation mail. And there it was: my 1992 Ford Taurus, just how I left it the day my Channel 8 photographer picked me up to shoot a story. He took me home after we finished, and that's where the car sat while I went on my trip to Germany. I was starting to worry about myself.

My good friend, Jim Scott, the assignment editor at WISH-TV, explained it to me. "Dick, you have a lot of files in your head, and sometimes a file gets lost or misplaced. That can happen to anyone."

This made me feel a lot better about things, so I told my wife what Jim said.

"Mary Ellen, I have a lot of files I have to keep track of. I'm no different than President Bush."

"Yes, dear, but the President has something for his files that you don't have: a cabinet to keep track of them."

7

ANTS IN THE PANTS

Big news in the world of medicine. It turns out that people who are couch potatoes spend more time on the couch than other people.

WOW! I always kind of suspected that, but no one wanted to pay me the big bucks for that information, so I kept it to myself.

The researchers recruited 10 mildly obese and 10 lean people to wear special underwear that used technology developed for fighter jets. Sensors were embedded in the subjects' undergarments, which then recorded their postures and movements every half-second, 24 hours a day, for 10 days. Apparently it wasn't hard to get people to volunteer for this. I think the idea of having jet controls in your underwear was one of the attractions.

They called this apparatus a "movement monitor," which intrigued members of AARP until they found out what it was really measuring. Maybe there will be another study for the kind of information they are looking for.

The study found that people who are thin spend a lot of time in their lives just puttering around, not necessarily doing anything constructive, but just puttering around.

I am a putterer, myself. Not a putter—a putterer. Just like someone who stutters is a stutterer, I am a putterer.

Now I find out that my puttering is the explanation for why a person like me, who can eat an entire pepperoni and sausage pizza, but who exercises very little, remains thin. Who knew?

According to the study, these movement monitors revealed that people can be divided into two groups: those who love to sit and those who are constantly moving.

My life has always been a moving experience. I seldom just sit. I eat standing up; I am on an exercise bike right now as I write this column; I read while walking up the stairs; I shake my leg up and down while at the dinner table or having a conversation with my wife. I check my e-mail 40 times a day, which involves going up and down the basement steps each time.

Of course, I do like to watch TV, but I never lounge on the couch. I'm either standing up in front of the TV, ready to change the channel, or running around the house looking for the remote. Or I'm looking for my cell phone. Or my keys.

I am the picture of hyperactivity. In the summer, hummingbirds gather at the window for inspiration.

My entire life, my mother, my wife, and my doctor have told me that my behavior was very troubling, that my nervousness would have a negative effect on my whole system, that it meant a shorter and less healthful life. "Calm down, relax," they would tell me. "You'll live longer." I'm glad I didn't listen to them. I'd be 400 pounds heavier by now.

Today I went outside and checked my mailbox several times to see if the mail had come. My neighbors think I am a bit strange. They just do not understand the aerobic benefit of this activity. I don't blame them for thinking it odd.

But what better way to spend a Sunday?

8

NEW YEAR'S STEVE

This is my New Year's Eve story. My wife thinks that simply by telling it, I expose myself as the cheap, unromantic, stick-in-the-mud, party pooper that I am. This is all true. But this is the 27th year in a row she has gone out with me. I mean, how hard up can she be?

For New Year's we went to a restaurant that offered what's called *prix fixe*, a fixed menu. Basically, that means that they were fixing to get rich, and I was fixing to complain about the prices for the rest of my life.

It has never been clear to me why a restaurant that has a glorious menu all year round with hundreds of items decides that one evening a year they are going to make you eat lamb shank and sushi whether you like it or not.

If I were in the restaurant business, my attitude would be: Hey, the year is just about done; I have all this tasty leftover stuff in the fridge; let's put it all out on a big buffet table and then start completely fresh on January 2.

At one point during the meal, I asked the waiter what I thought was a perfectly reasonable question—reasonable given the fact that I was about to pay more for an appetizer than I did my first Ford Pinto.

"Excuse me, Lionel, I don't like lobster bisque, so may I just have an extra endive salad?"

"Ummmmm, I don't think we can make that substitution. I'll check with Steve, the chef."

Ten minutes later, Lionel came back.

"Steve, the chef, says that substitution is not permitted."

Not Permitted? NOT PERMITTED! A green endive salad for a bowl of lobster bisque is not permitted? I once bought a car here in town, and after driving it for two days I told the owner of the dealership that it really didn't handle quite the way I expected. "No problem," said Rob, "bring it back and we'll substitute it with a Tuscon." Wow! Now that's what I call a substitution. An endive salad for a bowl of lobster bisque is *not* a substitution. Don't ever buy a car from a chef. In fact, I'm thinking of having dinner next year at the Butler Hyundai-Kia dealership.

The meal was a seven-course affair, which was more courses than I took my senior year at George

Washington University. And listen to this: The dinner New Year's Eve cost more than my entire academic semester in 1969. And that year I had a choice of *400* courses. There was no fixed menu at GWU... although I did try to substitute my Romantic English Poetry for Great American Novels the day before class started. The dean said that switch wasn't permitted. I don't know what happened to Dean Bissell. The rumor had it he went into the restaurant business.

When the bill came at the end of the evening, I took a quick glance, then used humor to cushion my shock.

"Lionel, I think you have mixed up our check for six people with that party of 20 over by the window."

"I don't think that is funny, Sir."

"You don't, Lionel? Maybe you should check with Steve, the chef."

The next day, I suggested to my wife that in 2006 we go out the night *after* New Year's Eve, thus having a better dinner at a cheaper price. I think this is a pretty good idea, but in all fairness to Mary Ellen, I think having Christmas morning on December 27 for the last 10 years is about as much adjustment as she can take.

I really think that $250.00 a couple for dinner was a lot of money. And that didn't include a 20 percent tip. Which makes me think everyone in that restaurant was stupid.

Except Lionel.

9

THE ART
OF HUMOR

Author's note: As I wrote this, Art Buchwald was in a hospice in Washington, DC. He wanted to spend his final days with friends and family. This is my memory of the one time our paths crossed.

From my very first day of college in September of 1965 at George Washington University in Washington, DC, I had wanted to meet Art Buchwald.

There was little progress on that front for almost two years, but then in 1967 I managed to convince the editor of the student newspaper, *The Hatchet*, to give me a weekly humor column. The feature, "Wolf's Whistle," became a hit, so much so that by the following year over 100 college newspapers ran the column each week. Many believed I was the first student syndicated humor columnist in the country.

That distinction provided the necessary courage to pursue my dream of meeting Mr. Buchwald. Being both headstrong and naive, I figured I could just look up his home number in the phone book. And there it was. Only much later in my life did I realize how unusual it was for someone of his stature to be listed. Don't try to look up Dave Barry's home phone number. Or Andy Rooney's.

Mr. Buchwald answered the phone and I nervously filled him in on my own "rich" history of writing humor columns. When I told him that I attended classes just a few blocks from his office on Pennsylvania Avenue, he invited me to come over one day for a short visit.

What a generous and uncharacteristic offer that was for someone of his celebrity. Even then, 35 years ago, he had already been one of the nation's top syndicated columnists for almost 20 years.

Two days later, I called Mr. Buchwald's secretary and explained to her that I had been invited to come to the office. "Yes," she said, "Mr. Buchwald said you'd be calling." I stammered, "He did?"

I entered Buchwald's office with a stack of *Hatchet*s under my arm. Buchwald stole a glance at me and snapped, "Let me see one of those newspapers, kid." He sat at his desk, put up his feet, ripped open the current issue, and began reading my column. I'd love to report to you that he burst out laughing. Instead, he just stared at the page, steely-eyed. Not even a smile. But I thought I detected a kind of subtle nod of the head that made me think maybe—just maybe—he saw a glimmer of potential.

After a few moments, he grabbed a pen off his desk and scribbled a few words over my byline. His phone rang and after he answered it, he grumbled under his breath, apologized that something had come up, and walked out the door. The entire meeting with him lasted but five minutes. I hadn't even had a chance to ask him what he thought of my stuff.

Dejected, I left his office.

I shuffled along Pennsylvania Avenue back to my apartment where I plopped down on the couch and opened the newspaper to the page that Buchwald had read just an hour before. I stared in delight at these words scrawled on the page:

"Wolfsie, stay out of my racket."
—Art Buchwald

I was only 21 at the time, but so far that was the coolest thing that had ever happened to me.

Days later, I cut out his signature and message and placed that part of the newspaper in a cheap black metal frame along with the photo I had snapped of Buchwald at his desk. It is still within eyeshot each week when I sit down to write my column.

Thanks, Art, for those two minutes. And thanks for all the laughs and smiles you have brought me and others. And please know this: I am now past 60, and that may still be the coolest thing that has ever happened to me.

When my tribute column appeared in local Indiana papers, several friends suggested I send the essay to the facility where Mr. Buchwald was spending his final days. *How presumptuous that would have been,* I thought, *imposing on a man cherishing time with close friends and family who, according to several news reports, were holding court daily.* As I write this, he is still surrounded by the rich and famous—politicians, journalists, and Hollywood celebs.

Oh, why not? I stuffed a couple of different newspapers that contained my Buchwald column into a large padded envelope and included a short note describing our brief encounter four decades earlier.

For the next few days, my mailbox became the watched pot that never boiled as I imagined receiving a reply. Finally, my sophisticated defense mechanisms took over, protecting me from disappointment. I simply forgot about the entire matter.

Last Tuesday night I was riffling through the mail. Bills, magazines, promotions, more bills. Then, what's this? A large envelope addressed to me. From Washington, DC. My tax refund? Not this year.

I ripped it open and out tumbled two newspapers, each one featuring my column—the one about Art Buchwald. And there, above my byline, scribbled in his very recognizable, but somewhat shaky handwriting, were the following:

To Dick Wolfsie: Anyone who writes a column about me, can't be all bad.
—Art Buchwald

And this, on the other newspaper:

To Wolfsie: Thanks for the column. Now I can die happy.
—Art Buchwald

And finally, typed on his letterhead with his signature:

```
To Dick Wolfsie:

I'm glad you went straight. I
figured you'd be sticking up 7-
11s.
```
—Art Buchwald

I don't know how I will display these treasures, how they will be framed or where they will hang in my office, but I do know this: Every time I look at them, I will be reminded that you should never underestimate the power of an act of kindness. A few brief minutes of Mr. Buchwald's time made my day. Heck, it made my decade.

He knows that, and I also believe he knows it's never too late to touch an audience—but without his regular column to write each day, he's just doing it one person at a time.

Art Buchwald passed away on January 17, 2007. His video obituary made available by *The New York Times* begins: "Hi, I'm Art Buchwald and I just died." Mr. Buchwald was 81.

10

PRICE OF INDEPENDENCE

I guess I shouldn't have been too surprised. It was Fourth of July weekend and the signs were everywhere. We were running some errands and suddenly my son's attention was diverted by something out his car window.

I will never forget his expression. His eyes widened; a visible lump appeared in his throat. He was transfixed.

"Dad, it's never affected me this way before. I guess I always took my freedom for granted. Now I realize how precious it is. It also makes me realize that nothing is free, that everything has a price."

"You are absolutely correct, Brett."

"Yes, Dad. In fact, everyone at school feels the same way. My American History teacher told me that when he first sees them every July he just breaks down and cries. I do have one teacher, Mrs. Francis, who says she wants to burn them."

"Why does she want to burn them?"

"She says they go up earlier every year."

"Well, Brett, that is the silliest thing I've ever heard. The American flag always waves on the Fourth of July."

"Dad, I haven't been talking about the American flag, I'm talking about that sign:

BACK TO SCHOOL SALE

He had a point. Here it was July Fourth and already Staples, Office Depot, and Wal-Mart were beating us over the head with premature reminders of the next school year beginning in a couple of months. When I was a kid back in New York, I bought my school supplies early in September, about two days before school started. This is not a good idea in Indiana, because if you wait until September 4, you won't find any Number 2 pencils for those mid-term exams on September 10.

I think there should be a law regulating how soon you can hype a holiday. For example, I like to pick out my Mother's Day cards at the last minute because my relationship with my wife is very mercurial. When the cards first came out the end of March last year we were in a very romantic period and I blew $27.00 on three goopy greeting cards full of double entendres. By the time May rolled around, things had cooled down a bit, but all those cards that show you appreciate your wife's cooking and sewing had been picked clean by other poor saps in a similar predicament. So there I was, stuck with those steamy sentiments from Hallmark. I hope I can time things better next year.

Same problem with Father's Day. When my son bought me a card at the end of April, I was his best buddy. By June, our relationship soured after he had been grounded for two weeks. But Brett was too cheap to buy new cards, so he just crossed out all the references to "World's Greatest Dad."

Yes, we always seem to be two months ahead of ourselves, which is why all shorts have been on sale since Memorial Day, swimsuits have been reduced 90 percent, and flip-flops are already out of season. Yesterday it was 90 degrees, and it was too hot to play golf, so I went over to Kohl's. They were all out of golf shirts, but that Christmas in July sale was a great opportunity to pick up a few turtlenecks.

11

PHONE HEX

Why do people always call me just when I have slumped over in my easy chair and slid into a dream about running away to Martinique with Charlize Theron? This is an important part of the day for me, and I am continually disturbed by people who call at such inappropriate times.

My phone, which can record a message or a two-way conversation, can store 100 phone numbers, and can identify the last 75 people who have called and hung up, does not have a switch to turn off the ringer. God knows I've looked.

Why not take the phone off the hook, you ask? Because some Einstein at Ameritech decided long ago that when you leave the phone off the hook, the receiver should emit a maddening wailing noise that gets progressively louder. So, if I were to take the phone off the hook to go downstairs and try to sleep in the crawl space with my head in one of those moldy suitcases, I'd still hear the phone.

Look, this is your problem, not mine, so I'm going to make this easier for you. Here's a handy little schedule you can tape to your fridge so you'll know the best time to call.

6 a.m.–9 a.m.: Don't bother. I'm at the office. The receptionist isn't there that early, and I can never remember my direct extension. My cell phone doesn't work inside Channel 8, and even if it did, I never remember to turn it on.

9 a.m.–10 a.m.: I usually get home from work about 9:07. This is when I have to deal with the incredible mess I made at 5:00 a.m. before I left for work. The milk is still on the counter, burnt toast crumbs litter the floor, and the remnants of overcooked scrambled eggs are clinging to the frying pan. I am in a very, *very* bad mood because I have to clean up my own filth. Call me later.

10 a.m. –11 a.m.: I usually make about 40 phone calls looking for story ideas around this time. My line is going to be busy. Not a good time.

11 a.m. –Noon.: This is just a terrible time to call. None of the people I tried to reach between 10 and 11 were there, so they are all calling me back now. This is apparently also a good time for the Marion County Sheriff's Department to call me for my lousy $25.00—for *what*, I don't know. They won't get it this year. I have been frivolously giving my money to the Red Cross and Salvation Army.

Noon.–1 p.m.: Hey, don't I get a lunch hour? I'll be cramming things down my throat. Illcalyabklter (that's *I'll call you back later*, with a salami sandwich in my mouth).

1 p.m.–3 p.m.: YES, THIS IS IT. THIS IS IT! THIS IS NAP TIME. **DO NOT CALL ME**. You should have called me earlier. Except Wednesdays, when I usually have to nap from 10 to 11 because of my weekly afternoon staff meeting. Or Fridays, when I'm so beat I'm usually napping by noon. Of course, on Mondays I have to stay at the office a little later in the morning, so that throws things off. Oh, and Thursday is my golf day, so don't call then. Except November through March.

3 p.m.–5 p.m.: This is when I watch cable news programs. First I check out CNN and listen to them bash Republicans. Then I tune into FOX News while they bash Democrats. You can call me between 3 and 5, but you have a 50-50 chance of catching me in a rotten mood.

At 5 p.m., I go home. Of course, I'm already home, but now it's officially the end of the workday, and I know you wouldn't want to bother me when I'm unwinding. After 5, I won't even take a call from my mother.

Come to think of it, I haven't heard from my mother in quite a while. She probably doesn't know a good time to call.

CHEAP FRILLS

My wife says it is a cheap compulsion and that no good can come of it. Sometimes I am away from my family for hours at a time. I can't help myself. Where do I go?

I go to the dollar store.

No matter how you slice it (and you can get a great knife there for a dollar), these are stores where you can buy anything for a buck. Anything, but your self-respect.

Of course, shopping at a dollar store is nothing to be ashamed of. But still, when I walk the aisles, eyeing the 64-ounce bottles of Lotta Soda and mega-size bags of cheese popcorn, I do wonder what people must be thinking about my store of choice. Are they commending me for my astute skills in discount shopping, or wondering if I am gainfully unemployed?

My addiction is very specific. Just like some find solace in a particular brand of whiskey, I am drawn to the dollar store on 96th Street in Fishers, Indiana. I mention this particular location because if you ever want to meet me in person, there's a pretty good chance you can find me there. Where exactly? I could be in the cookie aisle (60 ginger snaps for a buck), or the toothpaste section ($1 a tube), or the pet aisle (30 dog chews for a slim George Washington).

The manager's name there is Sheila. She is my enabler. But I hold no grudge. I accept all the blame for my weakness. It is not her fault that I will never eat that 24-ounce can of sardines. I can't blame Sheila for my purchase of six helium-filled balloons that say Happy 2nd Birthday. It's not Sheila's fault that I don't know one person who is turning two years old.

The psychology of shopping at the dollar store is dissertation material. Graduate students in marketing are wasting important time looking into the buying habits of Lexus owners and iPod purchasers. The bigger question is: Why would someone (me) buy three hammers just because they are a dollar?

I am going to start a support group. Here are my 12 steps to the recovery of self-respect:

1. Admit you are powerless to resist a huge $1 can of beets when you can't even stomach to look at the stuff.

2. Come to believe that a power greater than the supermarket can provide sustenance.

3. Make a decision to turn your shopping over to your saver.

4. Make a searching and fearless inventory of your shelf.

5. Admit to the exact nature of your spendthrift ways.

6. Recognize that lower prices are a higher power.

7. Humbly ask that the dollar store never become the Two Dollar Store

8. Love thy neighbor and share your faith in all that is good and wholesale.

9. Live a life where you no longer question the price of goodness, but know in your heart that the price is always a dollar.

10. Share your story with others, so they too can be savers.

11. Admit when you have strayed and that you once paid full retail for Cheerios.

12. Recognize the power of the almighty dollar and never take its name in vain.

I hope you will join my support group. There's a small monthly fee.

I think you know how much.

13

BUMMED OUT

Happy Anniversary, Carl Erskine.

Carl Erskine is a retired banker in Anderson, Indiana, who in October of 1955 was part of the Brooklyn Dodgers team that won their first—and only—World Series.

Carl was a part of my life growing up. As were teammates Duke Snider, Carl Furillo, and another Hoosier, Gil Hodges. And, of course, Jackie Robinson.

The Dodgers played at Ebbets Field in those days. The team's historic relocation to Los Angeles came two years after their victory over the Yanks. Had they finally beaten the Yankees as the Los Angeles Dodgers, it wouldn't have been the same. Trust me.

I didn't get much of a chance to go to Ebbets Field. Brooklyn seemed light years from our suburban home in New Rochelle, New York, some 30 miles away. Instead, I fell asleep six months of the year with a tiny transistor radio hidden under my pillow, praying for a home run by the Duke or another no-hitter by Carl (he had two). Often the games went past 11 p.m., which made getting up for school a real effort. My mom never knew why I dragged in the mornings. My father did but never said a word. Thanks, Pop.

Neither my father nor mother were huge baseball fans, but they were Yankee haters, a moniker one wore with great pride if you lived in the New York area. In those days, the Yankees were a curious combination of being the neighborhood rich kids and the schoolyard bullies. Things haven't changed much.

The Dodgers were the underdogs, Da Bums as they were called, and they were a team that any large city populated by a cross-section of religions and nationalities could easily embrace. It was for this very reason that the introduction of Jackie Robinson into baseball was perfectly suited for the Brooklyn Dodgers. It would have never worked with the Yankees. Trust me.

Although it has been 50 years, my memory is surprisingly vivid. On October 5, 1955, I was barely nine years old, but even then I knew the majesty of those hallowed words: seventh game of the World Series. This had traditionally been a time for Dodger fans to wring their hands and prepare for the inevitable. The Yanks and Da

Bums had faced each other what seemed like a hundred times in previous World Series. If the Dodgers had prevailed just once, I wouldn't be writing this story now. And Carl's anniversary wouldn't be so sweet.

I was seated on a brown floral chair in the dining room. The tiny TV had huge rabbit ears, but I remember that with a little fiddling, the picture became crystal clear. That picture, of course, was black and white, quite fitting because this was a battle between the forces of good and evil.

The chair seemed too comfortable so I perched myself on a mahogany coffee table and pushed it next to the television. Even then, I was not very good at dealing with tension. And on several occasions when the Yankees threatened (and they always did), I excused myself and retreated to my room until the peril had passed. I'm embarrassed to say that I still do that during Pacer games—more proof I have never grown up.

I would be a liar if I told you I had a distinct memory of each inning. I do remember a great catch by left fielder Sandy Amoros, and I recall being surprised that Duke Snider bunted in the fifth inning, given the fact the Duke was the top home-run hitter of the '50s. I understand it now, but the intricacies of baseball strategy eluded me in those days.

And, of course, I remember that final out. I even have a vague memory of Elston Howard flailing at the final pitch (a change-up, I have since learned) for the last, sweet out.

I sprang from the coffee table and let out a scream. I remember my mom and dad giving each other a hug. And I remember the Dodgers racing to the mound to celebrate their victory, just as every World Series victor had done generations before and 50 years since.

But this was different. I'm not sure I can convince you in this short essay, but it was different.

Trust me one more time.

14

THE WHOLE TOOTH

I had never read my own dental chart before. Being somewhat familiar with laws governing privacy, I pretty much assumed that what was going on inside my mouth was really none of my business. The government is very picky about these things. Once when I was in the hospital I called the nurse's station and asked the attendant how the patient in 407 was doing. She said he was recovering nicely, but she wanted to know who she was talking to. "I am the patient in 407," I told her, "and you're the first person who's given me any reliable information."

So the other day I was at my dentist's office and there's my chart sitting right smack in front of me. I had been getting bored with a 1989 issue of *Periodontist Monthly*, so I glanced at the folder and realized it was a running account of my mouth since l983, when I first came to Indy.

I've gotten pretty long in the tooth since then so I assumed there would be a pretty exhaustive detailing of all my choppers. What I didn't expect was the number of personal observations made by the dental hygienists over the years, remarks about me as a patient that were included in the permanent record.

Here were some of the notations along with a personal rebuttal, an opportunity I was not afforded at the time.

April 1987: Does not like to be probed

No, I don't. In fact, just last year when I was abducted by aliens, this funny-looking creature with six eyes said pretty much the same thing about me.

August l994: Has a small mouth

I found this odd, especially since it's in direct contradiction to all my references from previous employers.

February l998: Won't floss

This sounds like I had some hissy fit with the hygienist. It wasn't like that at all...

"Dick, you must floss."

"I won't floss."

"You will floss."

"Make me."

September 1998: Was a bit grumpy today

I had a glop of something in my mouth the size of a hairball, okay? A dental hygienist being upset because her patients are in a bad mood is like a professional burglar perplexed that he isn't more welcome in a new neighborhood.

June 2002: Doesn't talk much

Okay, I know this is a lame excuse, but when you have a fist, a pair of forceps, three balls of cotton, and a small vice in your mouth, you're just not in a chatty mood.

November 2004: Doesn't like dental videos

Gee, how can they say that? I even watched one about diseased, receding, bleeding gums. I thought it was a CSI re-run.

December 2005: Is tough to numb

It's about time they figured this out. Maybe that's why I've been screaming at the top of my lungs since April of '87.

The hygienist came in and caught me reading my own chart.

"You can't read that stuff. Certain parts of that are private."

"Wait a second, aren't those my private parts?"

I wish I had phrased that a little differently because apparently that is not the kind of thing you yell at dental hygienists. Considering the commotion I caused that day, I couldn't figure out why they agreed to keep me as a patient. Then I remembered the final notation:

January 2006: Pays promptly

15

This is great news for all of you out there who discovered a cheap place to buy gas and now have a few extra bucks to spend on your next vacation. A private company is making plans to whip people around the far side of the moon. The price: a snappy $100,000,000. I better say that in English. (I've never been good with more zeroes than you need to buy a used car.) That's one hundred million dollars.

According to the company's research, only 1000 people in the world can afford this, and 785 of those people would have to live at the YMCA if they got home safely. I'm no financial advisor, but if you are down to your last 100 million, you shouldn't be blowing it on some fly-by-night travel company with no track record.

With a fee like that, you can expect only people like Bill Gates, Warren Buffett, several Arabian sheiks, and two shortstops from the American League batting 240, to be able to afford this. My son saw this in the paper and asked me what chances he had to ever manage such a costly excursion. I wasn't optimistic. Even if he had kept his part-time job at Marsh as a bagger, at seven bucks an hour, he'd have needed to work the next 12,000 years without a day off. Of course, if he wanted a round-trip ticket, he'd have to moonlight, if you know what I mean.

I also wanted Brett to look at all the pros and cons of a trip like this. For example, I recently discovered that for my travels to Chicago, by the time I get to the airport, wait for the plane, fly to O'Hare, and take a taxi to my final destination, it's actually quicker to drive. I realized while explaining this fine point to my son, that I had chosen a pretty rotten example, but I don't think he was paying much attention, anyway.

You do have to imagine that the people taking this trip have been pretty pampered during previous vacations and might not be comfortable with the arrangements. Imagine Oprah looking into a seat on the aircraft…

"Let me understand this. For a hundred million dollars, I'm not even getting a window seat? Look, I don't want to sit on the aisle."

"Well, we don't have an aisle, Miss Winfrey. We just strap you into this tiny seat—three across—

and you pretty much sit there for the rest of the trip."

"Listen, I can get a flight just like that from New York to L.A. for a fraction of what you are charging. At these prices, how's the food? You know I'm on a diet and I am avoiding anything heavy."

"Oh, the food is very healthy. The snacks are so light they float right to the top of the spacecraft."

"How about frequent flyer miles? I figure that based on a 500,000-mile trip, I'm good for at least three free trips to the Caribbean when I get back."

"We don't offer those incentives, but we have decided to give our passengers five percent off on a future trip to Mars, dropping the price down to just under a billion dollars. That's the niftiest rewards program in the business. Plus, during our lunar stop, you get to sample the best cheese in the universe. Sorry, just a little moon joke."

I'm no Donald Trump, but if I am very frugal, sell off some of my assets, and max out my Visa card, I bet a can afford to do the moonwalk before Michael Jackson.

16

CLOTHES CALL

It's that time of year again and the dreaded day is not far off. Either September 27 or September 30. Sometimes it's October 3 or October 11. I never know what day it will actually be; I just get up one morning and I know it has arrived.

It's the day I take my summer clothes down to the basement and bring my winter clothes up to my bedroom. The first big issue is how to time this annual event. I usually wait until October, but last year I had some free time in September, so I tried to sneak it in and get it over with. I was pretty proud of myself until we had a hot spell. Then I felt pretty stupid at the neighborhood barbecue party in beige corduroys and a black turtleneck on an 85-degree day.

Every fall I also promise myself that I will wash or dry-clean all my spring and summer stuff so that when April 12 rolls around (or March 17, or April 23, or March 4), I can just go down to the basement and take everything fresh off the rack. This is an odd plan, since I don't have any racks in the basement. My golf shirts are hanging on the hot water pipes, my pants are stuffed in an old bureau drawer that has no handles, and my short-sleeve shirts have been deposited in a black plastic garbage bag in the crawl space. I would give some of the outdated clothes to a charity, but they're pretty musty, and I wouldn't want to create any ill-will down at Goodwill.

There are advantages to this clothing transfer. You get to learn a lot about your basement that you never knew. Just last year, when I was digging for my wool sweaters, I came upon an odd-looking thing on the wall that my neighbor said contains something called circuit breakers. I had never seen this door before because my pale blue leisure suits were draped over the metal box and had hidden it from view. Apparently, circuit breakers are generally not needed, but they are important in an emergency if things get too hot. That's the way I feel about my leisure suits.

This fall I found my tax records from l978 in a mildewed storage box on a top shelf behind three pairs of gray flannel pants stuffed in a torn lampshade. I remember that '78 was the one year I kept really, really good records, so I hope if I ever get audited by the IRS, they pick '78. I think I could impress them with my accounting acumen and classic fashion sense, especially if I wear those pants, which are also from '78.

I also found some high school term papers stuffed inside a pair of rubber galoshes. I read the first two or three essays and was impressed with what a good writer I was when I was in high school. Then I realized these were term papers I had assigned when I was a teacher and never got around to returning them.

In the future, I'm going to try to avoid this unnecessary transfer of clothes from one level of the house to another. This exercise is just a silly obsessive-compulsive action on my part and I will not yield to it next year.

I'll just live down in the basement.

17

FEEDING FRENZY

How much food are you supposed to bring to a potluck or a Thanksgiving get-together? The calculus of this must have stumped even Albert Einstein who came from a nice Jewish family where food, of course, played a very important role. Some biographers think the equation $E = mc^2$ really meant the amount of food you can Eat (that would be E) is equal to the size of the average Mouth (that's M) times the number of cousins (C) who were invited for a holiday dinner. Then Einstein's mother just squared everything, which has since become a holiday tradition and is why most people gain 11 pounds between Thanksgiving and New Year's.

Einstein has gotten a lot of credit for his theories on atomic energy, but very little recognition has been given to Mother Einstein's classic formula for how much potato salad to lug to the family reunion picnic.

This past Thanksgiving we were invited to my friends Bob and Cathy Haverstick's home. My wife insisted on bringing something so she could contribute to the sumptuous feast. "Bringing something" was always a risky thing when I grew up in New York. Whenever my mother brought something to someone's house, she would watch it like a hawk, concerned that her candied yams would go unacknowledged, thus requiring her to either chuck the remains at the end of the party or hide the half-filled casserole dish behind her back as she nervously slid out the door.

And there was a worse scenario. Suppose the dish was completely consumed. Not a scrap left. Wiped clean. That would have meant that my mother did not bring enough. She believed this miscalculation would stain the reputation of the entire Wolfsie clan. That's when my mother adopted Mama Einstein's theory of quantum food.

This made a huge impression on me as a kid. So when my wife offered to contribute her sour cream mashed potatoes to the Haverstick party, I tried to look at the decision about how much to bring in a scientific manner. Bob and Cathy were having 25 people for dinner, so we needed to make enough mashed potatoes for 50 people because if the spuds were that good, everyone was going to have seconds. But other people would also be bringing dishes. And these people, no doubt, were also familiar with this culinary formula. This meant that if all 25 people were bringing enough food for 50 people, there would be enough food on the Haverstick table that night to feed about 5,000 people. That would be plenty—even though Uncle Harold is a really big eater.

Dinner was quite wonderful, but getting all that food in the Haversticks' dining room was a problem. Guests were asked to leave their coats in the car so Bob and Cathy's king-size bed could be used as a buffet table for the 475 fluffy dinner rolls, 28 pounds of oyster stuffing, and 16 bowls of cranberry relish.

Sadly, at the end of the evening, many people felt the sting my mother used to experience when her string bean soufflé had been barely touched. As for Mary Ellen's sour cream mashed potatoes, I ate 12 portions. I don't like sour cream mashed potatoes, but the idea of my lovely wife coming home on Thanksgiving night clinging to the remains of an unappreciated casserole would have been too much for either of us to bear.

18

COMPLAINT DEPARTMENT

I love to write about the stuff that ticks me off. I have found through my work in the media that addressing a problem in the public eye will often result in positive change.

For example, I complained two years ago that it was unfair to pay $32.00 for a steak in a restaurant and then have to pay an extra dollar for blue cheese dressing. The column obviously had some effect because the steak is now $36.00 and the blue cheese dressing is $2.00. That's what I call power of the press.

I also complained about hotels that bill you $1.50 if you make your own coffee in your room. One hotel I had in mind has apparently dropped that charge due to my criticism, but their restaurant manager had never realized you can get away with charging extra for blue cheese dressing, so we're all pretty much back where we started.

Here are a few new complaints:

CEREAL BOXES: I can go into the dollar store and buy 50 zip-lock bags for a buck, but the skinflints at General Mills can't find a lousy two cents to put their Cheerios and Wheaties into a zippable plastic pouch inside their cardboard boxes. I know that there are many out there who think the current packaging is just fine. And that's not even counting100 billion tiny black ants.

VENDING MACHINES: The vending machine where I work, the change machine at the car wash, the soda machine in front of Sam's Club—none of them will accept my dollar bill. No matter how many times I stick old George Washington in there, it sticks it right back to me. I can use this same dollar to buy a newspaper or tip the pizza delivery man, but when I want a lousy package of Little Debbie doughnuts, what do I get but an attitude.

The worst part is when someone walks up behind me and says, "Here, Dick, try my dollar."

Of course, his dollar works right away, resulting in a snooty air as he reluctantly accepts my faulty bill and gingerly places it in a separate compartment of his wallet where it cannot contaminate the other currency. The result is a citywide rumor that I am making good money, and most of it is being made in my basement.

THE NAME OF MY STREET: I live on Narragansett Lane, apparently named after an

Indian tribe. I'd like to find the guy who picked this name and make him say it three times with my foot down his throat. Why couldn't he have named the street after one of his annoying daughters (Olivia sounds nice) or his Rottweiler, Rex, or how about that tree on the corner, Maple? When I purchase something over the phone, I have to say the street name and spell it three times. Then I have to listen while someone repeats it and butchers the poor thing to death. Sometimes people ask me why I would buy a house on a street with a difficult name like that. HUH?

Oh, and my house number is 2758, but there are only four homes on the entire block. What's with that? Come to think of it, maybe it is time to move.

ICED TEA: And finally, I want every waiter and waitress in Indiana to know that the next time I order an iced tea, I do not want it served with a thin slice of lemon desperately clinging to the rim of the glass.

YOU CANNOT SQUEEZE A SLICE OF LEMON; YOU NEED A WEDGE OF LEMON. NOT A SLICE, A WEDGE!!!!!!

Sorry I yelled, but every time I leave a restaurant I have tiny pieces of lemon flesh and pulp under my fingernails from trying to mush that sliver into my drink. Europeans may like a dainty tea decoration, but I think it's downright un-American. And I am a proud American, which is why I live on a street named after a famous American Indian tribe. I just wish it were Apache.

19

T his past weekend I watched my wife as she once again tackled a recurring problem with the same level of intensity and focus that she had brought to it before.

She took her usual measured approach, recognizing that one solution does not fit all. There was some trial and error in her method, but she knew that when she resolved the issue, everything would be a snap. The annoyance could be ignored no longer: None of our Tupperware had lids that fit.

I had also recognized there was a problem. You see, almost every leftover in our refrigerator is in a nifty little sky-blue plastic container with a piece of Reynolds Wrap over it. I think this is one of the reasons my mouth waters whenever I see aluminum foil.

I have never been to a real Tupperware party, but I am sure that the very idea of anything being topless would mortify these tight-lidded ladies. Their husbands, on the other hand, when hearing the word "topless," usually can't contain themselves, if you'll excuse a little Tupperware talk. I'd never go to one of these gatherings. Too many plastic people and too much burping.

This lid dilemma is mostly my fault. I always put the Tupperware tops on the bottom shelf of the dishwasher, and an hour later the result looks something like a Salvador Dali clock. There's a lady in Fort Wayne who has potato chips that look like famous people. I have Tupperware lids that look like Jimmy Durante, Karl Malden, and Walter Matthau.

Whoever invented Tupperware made the same mistake that the Heinz people made. And the same mistake as the Rubbermaid people made. Not to mention the Bic pen people. Tops (to everything) should be attached. I'm just glad the people at American Standard attach the lid to the commode. It's a good thing, or men like me who are always losing things would spend the first half of the day looking for the TV remote, then divide up the next 12 hours between the cell phone and the toilet lid.

"Mary Ellen, have you seen the lid to the toilet seat?"

"Did you misplace it again? When was the last time you used it?"

"This morning, moments after I brushed my teeth."

"Well, it must be there. Did you put it down somewhere? Come to think of it, you never put it down."

But getting back to my wife's little project in the kitchen. Personally, I thought the whole thing was a waste of time. "Why are you even bothering, Mary Ellen? Just throw out the misfits. We'll buy new Tupperware."

"Well, Dick. That is an odd position to take for a man who has 24 single socks in his bottom drawer."

Few things are harder to put up with

than the annoyance of a good example

—Mark Twain

"Mary Ellen, what's that hint of orange on all these containers?"

"That's just marinara sauce that won't come out."

"Well, if all those containers are stained and ugly, you really should throw them out."

"Boy, that sock analogy has still escaped you, hasn't it?"

It reached the point where I couldn't stand it anymore. The shuffling and rattling were disturbing my Sunday nap so I put my foot down.

"Mary Ellen," I firmly told her, "I want you to stop this silliness right now and do something more constructive."

She told me to put a lid on it.

20

DEATH OF A HANDYMAN

It's not easy losing a good friend, and it's even tougher when he's your handyman. I once told Steve he was the greatest fix-it guy east of the Mississippi. Steve said he could easily be the best west of the Mississippi, also. I think he considered moving to Utah just to prove his point.

Steve's approach to fixing things was methodical. He would analyze the problem, list the options, mull over those alternatives, formulate a plan, and fix the door.

Here's how I would approach the issue: Analyze the problem, list the options, mull over those alternatives, formulate a plan, and call Steve. As you can see, our approaches were almost identical.

I can never replace Steve as a friend, but I do have to find another fix-it guy. Over the past year, as Steve's condition worsened, my garage door fell apart, the molding on the kitchen door peeled off, the toilet seat broke, and the garbage disposal stopped working.

Because I was loyal to Steve and felt certain he would recover from his illness, I left things broken. Knowing Steve, I thought he'd be at my front door again very soon. Steve knew better. He was very practical and realistic about things. That's why he was such a good handyman.

I will miss Steve chiding me for being totally useless. When Steve fixed something, he made it look easy. But here were some of his favorite expressions while wielding a putty knife:

"It's a good thing you called me."

"Thank goodness you didn't try to do this."

"I got here just in time."

"You'd have paid twice as much for a plumber."

Now that Steve is gone, my wife fears I may try to fix something without professional help, which in the past has proven to be very costly.

"Can't you call someone?" she asked just the other day. "The hanging rod in my closet has been broken for a week."

"Who am I going to call, Mary Ellen? There will never be another Steve."

"Dick, you know everyone. That's what you do for a living—you meet interesting people. For example, don't you know someone who painted a baseball 20,000 times?"

"I do."

"Didn't you once interview a reptile ob/gyn?"

"Two of them."

"And what about the guest who had a collection of 3000 manhole covers?"

"A lovely woman."

"And the man who eats earthworms for his daily protein?"

"I had dinner with his entire family."

"And with all those contacts, all those people you know, an entire Rolodex filled with interesting, talented individuals, you can't find a handyman as good as Steve?"

"I don't think I can, Mary Ellen."

"I don't think you can either. We'll start looking for a new house tomorrow."

21

NOTHING TO BRAG ABOUT

This has never happened to me before. I have nothing to do. Really. Absolutely nothing. What a great feeling. I don't know where to put myself.

It's a Wednesday and it's pouring outside. I am home alone. I have edited all my stories for Channel 8 for the rest of the week. I'm two weeks ahead on my weekly humor column. No bills to pay. The dog has been walked. All my laundry has been folded and put away. I have absolutely nothing to do. AHHhhhhhhh! (You can read that anyway you want.)

"Dick, why don't you read a book or watch a movie on TV?" you might say. But you see, I read or watch movies when I do have something to do: that's my way of avoiding what needs to get done. If I read a book when I have nothing to do, what will I do when I really have to do something and I don't want to? I'm losing you, aren't I? Don't stop reading now. Do you have anything better to do?

I am so excited about this that I am going to brag about my situation. I think I'll call one of my busiest friends and rub it in. I know he'll be jealous.

"Bob, it's Dick. What are you doing?"

"Nothing, what about you?"

"Hey, that's exactly what I'm doing. And I thought I was the only one who was that lucky."

"Dick, when I say nothing, I don't really mean nothing. I'm paying some bills, doing some laundry, cleaning out the car. You know, nothing, really."

"You call that nothing? That's something. Don't you know anything about nothing? I am really doing nothing. I mean absolutely nothing."

"Look, are you bored? Do you want to come over here and do something together?"

"No, Bob, that's the whole point. I don't want to have anything to do with you."

"Well, you don't have to get nasty about it."

Enough of Bob. I wanted nothing to do with him. I tried another friend...

"Mikki, it's Dick. Guess what? I have nothing to do."

"So take a nap."

"A nap? You consider a nap nothing? A good nap is a commitment. An actual event. There's nothing like a good nap. But a nap is not nothing. Trust me. If I were sleepy right now, I would have something to do. Geez, can't I find one friend who knows something about nothing?"

I think I'll call my wife. Maybe she'd get a kick out of my state of affairs.

"Mary Ellen, it's me. I wanted you to know I am home right now and I have absolutely nothing to do."

"You're home in our house with a desk that needs to be cleared off, burnt-out light bulbs that need to be replaced, a basement that needs to be vacuumed, and winter clothes that need to be stored in the cedar closet...and you have nothing to do? I'd like you to get all that done before I get home tonight. I'm glad you called."

Boy did that backfire. Mary Ellen kind of put a damper on the whole darn day. Now, all of a sudden I have like nine things to do. I guess I better get started on my chores.

I might as well. After all, I have nothing else to do.

22

DEMANDING SCHEDULE

Have you been reading all this high-tech news about how in the near future we will be able to get all our TV shows either through an iPod (whatever the heck that is) or through the networks ON DEMAND? Apparently, ABC, CBS, and NBC will allow you to order up your favorite TV show and watch it any time, day or night, ON DEMAND.

So, if you don't want to watch *CSI* Tuesday night at 9:00 but you would rather observe someone bisect a dead person's spleen closer to dinner, well here's your big chance. Watch it when you want. ON DEMAND.

The very phrase is frightening to a guy like me who already suffers from a paucity of testosterone. I've been married for 25 years, and the only thing I ever got ON DEMAND in my house was an extra portion of broccoli. The phrase "I demand" is not the kind of verbiage that yields a lot of results in the Wolfsie home, so I'm skeptical of the terminology to begin with.

But let's get back to this TV show concept. I don't want my TV shows ON DEMAND. If I choose to watch *Desperate Housewives*, I think I should plop myself down in front of the TV set on Sunday night at 9:00 p.m. when the network says it's time, even if there is a pile of dishes in the kitchen that my wife is demanding I put in the dishwasher. (Hey, I guess there is demanding in my house, after all.) Of course, I could tape the show. I could also change the front axle on my car, but I know when I'm in over my head.

Why do I feel this way about ON DEMAND TV programming? Because every aspect of my life that I have any flexibility controlling never gets done. For example, I get *The New Yorker* magazine every week. I can read it anytime I want—and that is why there are 230 unread magazines going back well into the last millennium piled in my garage next to 340 *Newsweek*s and 150 Sunday *New York Times*. I'm going to read them all, I swear. I don't know when, but I'll do it when I'm good and ready. Which will be never. By the way, I've never missed an episode of *Lost*. What does this tell you?

Here's another example. I can change the filter in my furnace any darn time I want. But this was a big mistake on the part of the filter manufacturers. They should have said: Filters must be changed the first Thursday of every month at 7 p.m. or we take away your furnace and you freeze your butt off. People would put it on their calendars, work their schedule around the filter change, and maybe even have a neighborhood get-together to celebrate this lunar event.

But it doesn't work like that. You change the filter when you want to. When you have free time. That's why I haven't changed my filter in three years. That's why my family spends most of dinner wheezing instead of eating.

I don't want to watch *Survivor* when I feel like it. I want CBS to tell me when it's on and make me adjust my schedule accordingly. I need some structure in my life. We all do.

By the way, I'm getting a little tired of people telling me they haven't had a chance to read my column lately. From now on, I demand you read it every Tuesday at 4 p.m.

I know I have no right to insist on this, but trust me, you'll be glad I was so demanding.

23

DISAPPROVING NOD

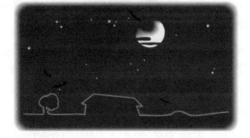

I received an e-mail last night from my brother-in-law who lives in Oregon. It was about 2 a.m., but I was still up so I responded to the message right away. He wrote back and said, "What are you doing up so late, Dick? Don't you ever sleep?"

I started to think about that and realized I never do sleep. To prove it, I kept track for one week, writing down how many hours of zzz's I got each night. I surprised even myself, so I thought I'd share this information with my wife, who has a very rigid routine when it comes to sleep: same time (10:30), same place (our bed), same TV station (the one with *Bonanza*.).

I guess she detected a hint of macho in my declaration and immediately took umbrage with my statement. I don't use the word umbrage a lot, so you can tell I was in for trouble.

"What do you mean you only slept 25 hours all last week? That's impossible, Dick."

"Whaddya mean? I'm very good with clocks and calculators. I kept track every night."

"Aha."

(This was a very bad sign. I have only gotten seven aha's in 25 years of marriage. In the interest of my own fragile ego, I will not list the circumstances surrounding each aha, but each one has been ingrained permanently in my mind. Let's say I want to buy some gadget from QVC that you hook up to the exhaust of your car and it melts the snow on the driveway in 10 minutes, and it costs $169.95. My wife just looks at me and says, "Aha number 2, Dear," and I quickly put my credit card away.)

Back to my time sleeping...

"So you think you counted all the hours, Dick? I mean every single one?"

"Of course! What kind of a dolt do you think I am?"

"Did you count the two hours you slept while waiting for Brett at his dental appointment?"

"I forgot those. Did I snore?"

"No, but you should thank the dental assistant for coming out every 10 minutes to wipe the drool off your chin. How about the time you were on the phone last week with your mother when she spent 60 minutes telling you about her health problems?"

"I don't remember that conversation."

"That's exactly my point. How about the birthday party we went to last week, and you fell asleep during the toasts?"

"Oh, yeah. And they were so nice to throw me a party."

"What about Saturday afternoon when you went downstairs to do the wash, and I found you with your head face down in the laundry basket?"

"I was looking for a missing sock, that's all."

"Then there was Mrs. Haberman's funeral; our backyard family barbeque; one time last week I don't think they'll print in a family newspaper, but it did very little for my ego; and at the checkout at Marsh Supermarket, which you might have gotten away with a little longer if it hadn't been the express line. I know you may argue with me about this but … Dick? Dick … Dick. DICK!!! Sweet dreams."

24

HOLY SWISS

A woman from Hollywood, Florida, recently made the news when she revealed that 10 years ago she was eating a grilled cheese sandwich and saw the image of the Virgin Mary in the bread. She just sold the item on eBay for $28,000. She claims it was whole wheat, but ya gotta figure it was Wonder Bread.

There is very little information about the buyer. In fact, no one is even sure if he is very religious or if he just loves cheese that's been aged a full decade, which, as you know, can get pretty pricey.

The very same story reports that when the woman made this supernatural discovery, she put the sandwich in a clear plastic box with cotton balls and placed it on her dresser for 10 years. I'm no social historian, but I think the old cotton ball theory of food preservation is pretty outdated. I'm guessing that after two, three months, that sandwich was pretty much history.

I am not criticizing this woman's religious beliefs; I just have to wonder why the forces responsible for this miracle would choose a grilled cheese sandwich. The Lord has revealed himself in some glorious ways, but a grilled cheese sandwich pales in comparison to a burning bush.

Why does stuff like this never happen to me? I've been staring at my lunch for 50 years, and the most I ever saw, maybe, was a very faint profile of Walter Matthau in an egg salad sandwich on rye, which I have been told would have gone for two bucks on eBay, assuming I got the sandwich to the buyer while it was still edible. Pumpernickel? You're looking at $2.50.

After I read about this story, I started paddling through my wife's beef stew but with little success. Then I bought a package of frozen vegetables at the grocery store, and when I opened it up I thought, for a brief moment, that I saw Jeff Gordon in the carrot, cauliflower, and green bean medley. But once the glob started to thaw, it honestly could have been any racecar driver. So I just ate it.

I do believe you can find celebrity images in Jell-O, but once what I thought was Pat Sajak and Vanna White in the cherry-flavored variety, was just my own reflection with my wife standing behind me laughing.

The problem with a story like this is that people who are looking for a quick buck on eBay will start imagining these culinary apparitions. It's one

76

thing to look into the clouds and see Mickey Mouse; it's quite another to start telling people you saw Jessica Simpson in your eggplant parmigiana.

For many years, Myrtle Young of Fort Wayne, Indiana, has amassed a collection of potato chips that resemble celebrities like Snoopy, George Bush, and Yogi Bear. She recently complained that she's been having a heck of a time finding new additions. Her daughter, who supplies her with chips, had been substituting with Pringles from the dollar store.

Well, that's it for this column. My wife ordered a pepperoni and sausage pizza for dinner and it just arrived. I'm not really hungry, but it's fun to see new people.

25

FEELING BLUE

Every few days when I pull into the gas station, I gaze at the prices and start to worry. I remember when it used to be so much cheaper. Now the price has crept up to the point where I have to be more frugal. I'm not so quick anymore just to waste the stuff. I use it wisely and only when it is absolutely necessary.

Just the other day I traveled all over town to see if I could get a better price. I'm one of those people who believe that all the brands are about the same, so it's just a question of who is selling it cheaper.

For a while, I actually stopped buying the product, but how long can you go without it?

I see things much more clearly now.

I'm sure you feel exactly the same way about your windshield washer fluid.

The other day wiper fluid hit $1.99 a gallon. I'm glad they don't do that 9/10 of a cent silliness because I refuse to stand in line behind some crazy person who wants change from her two dollars.

I've never been real successful with washer fluid. Once I open the hood of the car, any place that can accept liquids is fair game. I guess I've put the solution in the wrong receptacle several times in my life. But as a result, I have learned a few things about cars that you (or Click and Clack on NPR, for that matter) may not even know. For example, you cannot substitue windshield washer fluid for power steering fluid if you have any plans to make turns. Nor is windshield washer fluid an effective antifreeze alternative. However, the people at Edward's Transmission will be very sympathetic: They'll try to tell you that you are not the first person to make this mistake…but one in 100,000 did not make me feel any better.

Even if I find the right place for the fluid, the whole windshield washer thing has always been a problem for me. I've owned dozens of cars in my lifetime, but I have never felt that I have gotten a really good spritz from both nozzles. My old Ford, for example, has a right spray nozzle that dribbles like the last shot of mustard in a squeeze bottle. But the left sprayer could put out a second story

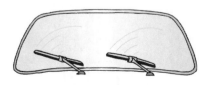

blaze if I parked the car under the bedroom window of my house.

My other problem is that I am already easily distracted when driving a car. (Last week I swerved to avoid a pine tree, and it was actually the car freshener hanging from the rearview mirror.) As a result, I try not to focus on the liquid as it cascades down the windshield. Sometimes I forget about the semis or senior citizens in front of me.

As I stare out my windshield I wonder if switching to plain old water wouldn't be cheaper and just as effective as wiper fluid.

For some reason, I always go back and forth on the issue.

26

SNOOZE ALARM

I can't believe I missed this story in the news-paper. I must have been sleeping. Wait—that's exactly what I was doing. This is apparently a pretty good excuse, according to Arshad Chowdhry, the inventor of a new and convenient way to nap.

Mr. Chowdhry says he comes from a sleepy family, which explains his first name. It was supposed to be Arthur, but the doctor woke his father in the middle of a nap in the delivery room to ask the newborn baby's name and Arshad was all he could manage to spit out.

Mr. Chowdhry, a New Yorker, said he was tired of seeing people sleeping in bathrooms and in their cars. Actually, Mr. Chowdhry was just tired in general, which is why he invented MetroNaps, a high-tech enclosure where people can take a quick snooze in the middle of the day.

Mr. Chowdhry charges you $14.00 for this nap and there's no guarantee you'll fall asleep. Some people just vegetate with their eyes wide open, doing nothing—something you could do at work while getting paid.

By the way, when Mr. Chowdhry started to market his idea, he discovered a lot of people snoozing in the bathrooms at Grand Central Station were not suffering from daytime sleepiness, but from homelessness, which is why, in the spirit of a true New York City humanitarian, he dropped the price from twenty bucks to just fourteen.

It still seems like a waste of money. What's wrong with just dozing at work? Every afternoon for 25 years, when my brother wanted to catch 40 winks, he simply slouched in his chair, and he never had a problem nodding off. He had a problem keeping his jobs, of course, which is why he's now a New York City cab driver. Not only is he napping better, but he gets better tips because he's not always yakking at the people in the back seat. However, passengers on their way through the Lincoln Tunnel find his snoring a bit disconcerting.

Mr. Chowdhry did extensive research and determined the most profitable place to put his business was at airports. I'm no graduate of the Kelley School of Business, but I'd like to ask the 2500 people at the Vancouver Airport who each shelled out $14.00 to Mr. Chowdhry last year, if it ever dawned on them to nap on the plane during their 20-hour trip from Sydney.

I know what you are saying: Dick, it's hard to go to sleep on a plane. AHA! There's your problem. No one is asking you to go to sleep on the plane; we're talking about napping. Going to sleep and taking a nap are as different as lightning and the lightning bug, a comparison I am stealing from Mark Twain while he is not using it.

According to Chowdhry, it is mostly men who nod off in his enclosures. Women won't nap. They are afraid they're going to miss something. Like a sale, or a beautiful sunset, or the plot of a movie. Men don't care about stuff like that. If my wife falls asleep during the day, she awakens with an apology and an explanation of her behavior. "I don't know what happened! I must be coming down with something." Men have a different attitude when finishing a short slumber: "Wow, that was a good nap. No, that was a *great* one. You know, I'm becoming quite the expert at this."

Male or female, everyone likes to take advantage of a good promotion. That's why Mr. Chowdhry offers frequent dozing miles. Take 20 naps in one of his cubicles and earn a free one. Or, for 10 naps you can upgrade from coach to couch, with a free teddy bear and blankie.

27

FIGHTING WORDS

LONDON - A woman who keeps quiet during an argument with her husband is four times more likely to die from heart disease.

This is all according to a study published in a journal by the American Heart Association, a publication I don't read—but I really don't have to because the information always ends up in *USA Today* so it can drive more men like me nuts.

So, let me understand this. If I argue with my wife, I'm a boorish brute and a sexist. But if she wants to argue with me, she'll live longer. Ain't research great?

This is the same newspaper that just revealed to the public that drinking a couple of cups of coffee a day is good for your health, only months after they said coffee caused heart disease. For a long time, they said it was tea that was good for you, so now I'm drinking both tea and coffee four times a day, just to be sure. I'm not convinced I will live longer, but since I can never fall asleep, it will certainly feel longer.

Just last night my wife and I had a pretty big disagreement. While she was yelling at me I swallowed several cups of espresso.

"Dick, we're having a debate, and instead of defending yourself like a man, you just keep gulping down more coffee."

"Do you think you're the only one who wants to live to be 100?"

My wife and I have argued about some odd stuff over the years. "Argue" is probably a bad choice of words because Mary Ellen always reads my columns before they go to the newspapers. She thinks if I tell people we argue, the public will assume we don't get along. We talked about this the other day. Our voices got louder; we shook our fingers at each other. In the end, I would have said I lost the argument, but now I know I simply got annihilated in the "discussion."

Truth is, we have debated just about everything in our 25 years of marriage: how to eat popcorn, when to nap, how to load a dishwasher, how to cook a scrambled egg. We once debated whether my mother knew how to raise children. I thought my mom had done a pretty good job, but I must admit Mary Ellen provided some very strong proof to the contrary. Of course, I was the proof.

(At least I'm impressed with good evidence when I see it.)

I must not be a very good debater because I seem to lose the exchange even if I have most of the facts in my favor. For example, I was pretty sure this past July was my wife's 54th birthday, but she thought it was closer to 52. I presented her passport and her driver's license to bolster my position.

"Not only that, Mary Ellen, but I'm 60 and I remember when we got married I was four years older than you."

"Oh, Dick, you're living in the past. That was more than 25 years ago."

I hope the two of us have many more heated discussions. I figure if she keeps yelling at me in order to stay healthy, we can endure another 30 years of pure marital bliss—as long as I keep guzzling coffee.

I know you're tempted to say, "Wouldn't that be grounds for divorce?"

You should be ashamed of yourself.

28

ONE FINAL STEP

1 0,000 steps a day. That's what the NASEWA (National Association of Something Else to Worry About) is now recommending. They said that the average person walks only 1000-3000— and they suggest taking *10,000* steps a day. Apparently, 10,000 steps a day is equivalent to walking a few miles, something most people won't consciously do, but the trend nowadays is apparently unconscious exercise, which I have always preferred, anyway.

The only thing you need to buy is something called a pedometer, a tiny gadget that hooks on your belt and measures every step you take, every move you make, every bond you break. Oops, sorry. I think that was a song by Sting.

If you read the literature you discover that the advocates of this program have a major marketing problem. They want you to walk more, but they don't have a clue where they want you to go. In fact, they admit they don't care where you go or what you do when you get there. Apparently, it is just the act of going that is important. This is not a new idea. The entire system of higher education is based on this concept.

I told Sidney, my chubby ex-brother-in-law in Ohio, about this idea and he was pretty excited to find a program that gave the consumer so much flexibility. But he was concerned that it was doomed to failure like Hillary Clinton's health care program because it involved the same number of steps, 10,000.

I asked Sidney to keep track of his steps each day and I convinced him to buy a pedometer, which was a hard sell. Except for that new bucket of KFC with all three kinds of chicken, Sidney is usually cautious about buying anything new and untested.

I got a note from Sidney the other day bragging about the 1700 steps he had racked up on his pedometer in the first day, which is quite a bit short of 10,000, but more than I expected. Sidney even wrote down where he walked to get to his first day's total. Here's his letter and analysis.

Dear Dick,

I managed to go almost 2000 steps the other day. I could hardly believe it because I don't consider myself a health nut.

1. Walked to the mailbox to get the pound of imported chocolate I ordered from Switzerland.

2. Went up and down the basement stairs to steal one more scoop of Ben and Jerry's Cherry Garcia from my son's container in the fridge.

3. Walked from the living room where I take a nap to the bedroom to get a good night's sleep.

4. Walked from the pro shop to my golf cart.

5. Walked into the garage to get on my riding lawn mower.

6. Walked to my office (hey, it's not my fault I work out of my house).

7. Walked from my space in the parking lot to the escalator in the housewares store up to the second floor to buy a new hammock.

I hate to disappoint a liberal like you, Dick, but despite this effort I haven't lost a single pound yet. Just one more example of a government program that doesn't work.

However, I do want to thank you for introducing me to the 10,000-step program. It's the most exercise I've gotten since I walked out on your sister.

29

The big medical news this month is that eating fish at least once a week is good for your memory. I don't know how this can be big news. They've been calling fish "brain food" for 50 years.

Of course, researchers also told us last year not to eat a lot of fish because most of it is contaminated and if you eat too much you will glow in the dark. I guess this year's researchers forgot that.

I don't believe this memory thing at all. When I was in high school I ate fish sticks three days a week and tuna sandwiches on weekends. Then I went to college where I spent half my waking hours looking for either my car or my spiral notebook. So much for the memory theory.

However, when I was a junior in college I used to go down to this pub every Friday night and eat crab cakes and drink six bottles of beer. I do have a distinct recollection of getting thrown out of the bar several times, so maybe there is something to this memory thing after all.

Now 40 years later as I enter my golden years, I get a little perturbed about all this talk about memory loss, especially in older people. I'm no rocket scientist but it seems to me there is a logical explanation for all this supposed forgetfulness. Think of your head as a jar (this may be tough for those of you who are metaphorically challenged). Inside this jar are pieces of memory—beans.

My theory is that you can only get so many beans in that jar. For argument's sake, let's say 568,777,879,575,001 beans will fit in your jar. That last bean is your memory of where you just put down your reading glasses. Sadly, your jar is now out of space. This is a problem because your wife calls and says "Don't forget to turn off the stove before you leave to go fly-fishing." But that bean won't fit. Uh oh.

As you age, your jar fills up. You are not losing your memory; you just have to get rid of a bean if you want to put in a new one in. When you are young, there's room for several cans of beans, so your head can keep stuff in it that you have absolutely no use for. That's why when you are 35, you can go to a party and remember the host's name even after two frozen daiquiris.

When you near 60, you've got to make some important choices. Let's say you still want to remember that glorious night you spent with

Gladys at Club Med in 1964. Okay, fine, but that means you're going to go downstairs to get a roll of toilet paper and come upstairs with two pork chops from the freezer. You may not want to face this, but it may be time to say adios to the memory of your love fest in Martinique...or go without toilet paper.

Is this starting to make sense?

The bottom line is if you hate halibut, flounder, tilapia, and mahi-mahi, there is no reason to force yourself to eat it. Your memory will be just as good if you eat at The House of Ribs as if you dined at The Salmon Shack.

And don't you forget it.

30

COOKING WITH GAS (OR CHARCOAL)

Mark Twain was right when he said: "There are three kinds of lies: lies, damned lies, and statistics." You'd like to think that there are dedicated people out there doing some great work in the field, people who realize that a well-founded statistic is a precious stone that needs the proper setting. (Hey, that was pretty good.)

Here is a statistic just released from the people who make Blue Rhino propane tanks. Brace yourself. This makes any silly number about global warming just so much fear-mongering. Here it is:

69.3 percent of men vs. 66 percent of women prefer gas grills to charcoal grills.

And just when you have caught your breath; just when the import of these numbers has been indelibly forged into your psyche like a hot coal in the palm of your hand, this: 83 percent of men and 79.7 percent of women agree food tastes better when prepared on a grill.

What could possibly account for this vast taste variance of 3.3 percent between men and women? I have always accepted the statistical difference between the sexes when it came to libido, spending habits, and consumption of dark chocolate. Those disparities were understandable, even obvious on their face—especially the chocolate one. But the 3.3-percent gap in the appreciation of gas vs. charcoal grills is just inexplicable.

The folks at the International Genome study probably never took the time to see if there was, indeed, an actual gene to explain this discrepancy. They found one for selfishness, social ability, even promiscuity, but not a blessed second has been spent on charcoal vs. gas grills. You laugh (I hope), but this is your tax dollar squandered by the government. Your money up in smoke— especially if you prefer charcoal.

It is times like this that I lament the death of Einstein. Oh the hours he wasted with electrons and gravity, time and space…it all seems so trivial, relatively speaking.

I decided to do a survey on my own block just to see if the results meshed with the typical American neighborhood. I knocked on the first door.

"Hi, Mark, I'm just taking a little survey. Do you prefer a charcoal or a gas grill?"

"Well, that's kind of a touchy question in this house. I prefer gas, but Cathy likes coals. I'd rather not go on the record with this, though. Our kids are still in school, and we belong to a very conservative church. That's just the kind of dirt about this family I'd like to keep between us. Would you like to know about our sex lives or how much in debt we are?"

I tried one more house….

"Norman, I just dropped over to find out whether it makes any difference to you whether you grill with gas or charcoal."

"It meant a lot to the first Mrs. Collingwood; that's why there's a second Mrs. Collingwood. I knew we could handle the fact we were different religions. And we managed to deal with my view that we should have 12 children and she hates kids. Compromise is important in a marriage. Ask my six boys. But gas vs. charcoal? There's only so much you can do to make a relationship work."

I want to thank the Blue Rhino people for opening my eyes to this cultural divide. Oh, one last note from the people at Blue Rhino, another nugget of truth that will fascinate you. This is exactly what the research said: 36 percent of grillers don't know they're out of propane gas until they're actually out of propane gas.

That's funny…that same percentage of my readers don't know they're at the end of my essays until they've read the last word.

31

The big news recently was that new research has shown eating a high-fat diet does not necessarily lead to heart disease, cancer, or stroke. It does lead to Wendy's, Hardee's, and McDonald's.

The morning news shows were quick to round up their resident doctors who were all at Starbucks sipping black coffee and choking down sawdust-flavored scones. Doctors also eat at real restaurants, but don't even think about getting a Heimlich maneuver from one of these professionals at Bubba's Steakhouse, because no self-respecting cardiologist is going to abandon his 32 oz. rib-eye and reveal to the world the carnivore that he is.

"This study should not be taken as permission to eat a lot of high-fat foods," said Dr. Tim on *Good Morning America*. "Let's not jump to any conclusions based on this research," he continued, angry he had given up Chinese spare ribs based on some wacko experiment one of his classmates did at Harvard Medical School 30 years ago.

The food police are telling you this study should be taken with a grain of salt (even better, salt substitute). They are in denial because the results are not consistent with their preconceived beliefs. This is a very bad way to make a decision. I sure hope President Bush is reading this.

I think the problem here is that the medical community is wasting money on inane studies while TV stations are doing the important research. That's right, TV stations. The Discovery Channel just completed a series of tests to confirm what has been considered a bedrock of American eating habits: The Five-Second Rule.

Yes, long before the eight glasses of water a day declaration, years before the no-double-dipping decree, and decades prior to the warm mayonnaise scare, people were comforted knowing that any food item hitting the floor and picked up in less than five seconds retained its purity and could be safely consumed.

But is it true? Apparently my beagle thinks so. If an entire pot of spaghetti fell to the floor, Toby would snarf it up before the five-second threshold. Dogs are smart that way. Even a beagle knows a kitchen floor is a dirty, filthy, disgusting harbinger of germs, bacteria, and disease.

And to think, I walk on one almost every day.

The professor who assisted in this research begins the Discovery show by clearly stating the five-second rule is not scientifically accurate. Germs do, in fact, form on food before five seconds. The introductory remarks were intended to engage the viewers and prevent them from waltzing over to *Dancing with the Stars* on another network. I know the tease worked for me. "So, the five-second rule is not true," I thought. "Then how many seconds do I have? Three? One? Oh, joy—maybe you have *more* than five seconds!"

Apparently not. The research showed that you would be better off recouping your food from a toilet seat than from the kitchen floor, which is sure good information to have. I guess.

Dry foods, by the way, are safer than wet foods if you drop them. I mention this so that if you should drop a piece of buttered toast on the kitchen floor, take careful note which side it lands on, then act accordingly. I'll tell you right now, it almost always lands butter side down.

They proved that on the Food Network.

32

HAPPY ANNIVERSARY

2006 marked my 25th anniversary in television and radio. If you have absolutely nothing better to do, read on. I'd like to share with you some of my favorite moments.

THE MOST FRIGHTENED I'VE EVER BEEN:

In 1980, in Columbus, Ohio, I was the first person to interview G. Gordon Liddy when he got out of prison. After he gave me 10 one-word answers, I took a bold step to make the interview come alive...

"Have you ever murdered anyone, Mr. Liddy?"

Mr. Liddy stared directly at my neck. I broke out in a sweat.

"Only an idiot would expect me to answer that question, Mr. Wolfsie. But I have been trained to kill a human being with a fountain pen in less than a second."

Before I could stop myself, I found myself reaching across and removing a Bic pen from his outside coat pocket. The first smile of the night came to his face. Looking back, it's probably one of the dumbest things I've ever done. And the coolest.

FUNNIEST THING MY WIFE EVER SAID AFTER A SHOW:

Almost 25 years ago, I did a segment in Columbus about couples who swing. This isn't dancing. These are married folks who, how can I say this nicely, switch partners. My wife sat aghast in the audience that night as she listened to this very adult discussion. After the show she told me how impressed she was.

"You're impressed?" I asked, jaw dropping.

"Yes. We can't even find people to go to the movies with."

BIGGEST THRILL:

In 1982 I interviewed my idol, Steve Allen. He was talking about the great comics of the silent era…

"Chaplin was my favorite, but where do you find people of that ilk any more?" asked Allen, rhetorically.

"You could join the Ilks Club," I suggested, realizing this was a totally rotten pun. But one that Allen might have made himself.

Steve Allen cackled, as only Steve Allen can. I had made my hero laugh. Several years ago when

Steve Allen appeared in Indianapolis, I interviewed him and I reminded him of the story. Not that I thought he'd remember, but I wanted him to know how much that had meant to me.

DENSEST CALLER OF MY RADIO CAREER:

When I was on WIBC doing a political talk show, a man called to express his antigovernment view...

"I hate the government. They never do anything right. The less government, the better. We'd be better off if they would just shut down."

"What do you do for a living, Sir?" I asked.

"Nothing. I'm on Social Security."

"How do you pay your medical bills?"

"I have Medicare."

"Did you go to college?"

"Yeah, on the GI Bill."

"How'd you buy your house?"

"I got an FHA loan. Say listen, Wolfsie, what the heck does this have to do with how much I hate the government?"

MY BEST PUN:

In the late '70s, I was hosting *Good Morning, New York*. I had the opportunity to interview boxing champion Sugar Ray Leonard. Because he was doing Seven Up commercials at the time, I asked him if he would mind autographing a 2-liter bottle for me while we were on the air talking.

"But, Dick," he said, "this is a regular Seven Up bottle. I just do the Diet Seven Up commercials."

"Okay, could you sign it 'Sugar-Free Ray Leonard'?"

Well, that's it. You are probably saying how incredibly self-serving this story was. Yes, indeed. It was an anniversary present. To me. From me.

LEFTIST PROPAGANDA

It was the best of dinners. It was the worst of dinners.

The Wolfsies were invited to our friends, the Haversticks', for Thanksgiving. On the surface, this promised to be a welcome break from our long tradition of dining alone. Our family is small, which means the festivities sometimes lack the joyfulness of a larger get-together.

We had a terrific time, of course. Good food and good people made for a wonderful evening. But that next morning my wife and I awoke with an uneasy feeling that had settled in our gut—not to be blamed on Cathy's scrumptious oyster stuffing. No, it was something else.

"Dick, I am experiencing a lot of regret this morning. I think we both know why."

"I suspected this might happen, Mary Ellen, when we decided to join our friends for Thanksgiving dinner."

"But, I never thought it would affect us this way. How will we ever get through this week?"

"Yeah, I know, Mary Ellen: No leftovers. We have no leftovers."

Just the utterance of those words was so disconcerting that my wife and I simply stared at each other for a few moments until the reality set in. We couldn't look forward to a week of dry turkey sandwiches, turkey a la king, and cranberry relish ambrosia. It was too much to bear. I swallowed my pride and called Bob.

"Bob, it's Dick. Thanks so much for dinner last night. Listen, do you have any leftovers...uh, you know, left over?"

"Excuse me?"

"Mary Ellen and I noticed that there was a fair amount of turkey still on the platter and, no offense, but that green bean casserole wasn't quite the hit it deserved to be, so we were just wondering..."

"Look, Dick, this may come as a shock to you, but to the dinner provider go the spoils—not that anything has spoiled, but I think you get the picture."

"Well, what happened to your holiday spirit?"

I hung up the phone and realized that I was not alone facing this predicament in the post-

Thanksgiving world. Many people go to their family's and friends' for holiday dinner, only to come home that night unprepared for the next 10 days. Lacking provisions, they haunt supermarkets and convenience stores, trying to piece together what might pass for a potluck supper. No self-respecting person cooks a dinner that Friday night. Some sneak out to Cracker Barrel, but they sit in the dark corners with a copy of the *Farmers' Almanac* hiding their faces.

My friend, the late radio personality Dave Koffee, once joked about opening a place called Leftover City, where Thanksgiving dinner guests could purchase quarter-casseroles of candied yams, half-eaten crescent rolls, a pint of cold oyster stuffing, or chunks of crumbled pumpkin pie. Hmmm...not so crazy after all.

Next year, I think I'll invite the Haversticks to our house for dinner. And when they leave that evening may their hearts and stomachs be filled with the blessings of the holiday season.

And may their hands be empty as they go off into the night, knowing that the next morning they, like the Wolfsies this year, would soon be filled with despair. They would face an after-Thanksgiving Friday morning breakfast of scrambled eggs—without giblets, Waldorf salad, and cranberry relish on the side.

34

DUMB DUMB

I would like to report some of the dumbest stuff I have read about in the news.

The NFL has just decided to put luxury throne-like seats on the sidelines at Gillette Stadium in Foxboro, Massachusetts. They want the fans to feel more a part of the game.

I think this is a wonderful idea because after the melee in Detroit, there was some concern that the athletes had to travel too far to punch the fans, so the players' union is advocating seats right on the field. This is also beneficial to the fans who have been complaining that if they are going to be assaulted, they'd like to just get it over with, go to the emergency room, and be home in time for *Jerry Springer* re-runs.

Scott Suprima, who works for Seating Solutions, designed the seats and admits that they may have to construct a canopy to protect the patrons who paid big bucks for this option. Suprima's company was concerned that people in the luxury seats might be mistaken for athletes by people in the cheap seats and get hit by a chair.

By the way, according to *USA Today*, there will also be plasma TVs next to the seats, which I am assuming is for blood transfusions.

Here's another gem: A new government regulation states that you are not allowed to smile when having your passport or driver's license photo taken. As it was described in the newspaper, "the machine can be flummoxed by smiles, which introduce teeth, wrinkles, seams, and other distortions."

First of all, I never thought of my smile as introducing my teeth. I usually just say hello to people, and if they want to get friendly with my teeth, they'll just have to make their own introductions.

And as far as wrinkles go, we all have them. Seams, I'm not so sure about. What is a seam? I've always thought of my face as pretty seamless, but I want to thank the U.S. Government for giving me yet another thing to worry about since 9/11.

Plus, it ticked me off that I had to look up "flummoxed" in the dictionary.

Of course, once again we have another silly, unnecessary regulation. I've been to the Bureau of Motor Vehicles hundreds of times and have never seen people voluntarily smiling, to begin with. In fact, if you ask people to smile for their BMV photo, they'll rant for 20 minutes on why they can't think of anything to be happy about. Then they'll take a ticket and sit for another two hours waiting for the picture.

And, as far as passports are concerned, remember the words of Mark Twain: If you look like your passport photo, you're probably too sick to travel.

How about Fandango? This is the much-ballyhooed new way to buy a movie ticket. Instead of standing in line at the movie theater, you go online and buy your tickets over the Web. Is that a great idea, or what? No, it's the dumbest idea in the world. You get this print-out and then you take it to the theater and stand in the very same line as the people who have not discovered this incredible service. It doesn't save you *one second* of time. Not one. In fact, it takes more time because you have to go on the Internet to download a receipt that gives you permission to stand in line and pay for the ticket like every other loser who is waiting.

35

In the car last week, I reminded my wife that I was about to get hit with another birthday.

"Well, Mary Ellen, I'm going to be 58. I guess I'm getting pretty old, aren't I?"

"Don't be silly, sweetheart; 58 is still very young."

"Maybe, but you know… in only 12 years I'll be 70."

"Whoa! I never thought of it that way. You are getting up there."

"By the way, dear, in 16 years you'll also be 70."

"That's totally different. Sixteen years is a very long time."

The truth is, I don't like birthdays. If I never had another one, that would be OK with me, but the implications of that are pretty serious.

Let's just say this: If 14 waiters never again sing "Happy Birthday" to me in a restaurant full of strangers while I'm trying to choke down a bowl of clam chowder, that would be fine in my book.

My mother, who is 86, also has a problem with accepting her advancing years. For my entire life, she has said the very same thing to me on my birthday, only she continually updates it.

"I can't believe I have a son who is 56."

"I can't believe I have a son who is 57."

"I can't believe I have a son who is 58."

She seems genuinely surprised each year, but this annual mantra started when I was a toddler. Crying to the neighbors, "I can't believe I have a son who is seven years old," never garnered the sympathy she craved.

I do hope that someday my mother will be able to say, "I can't believe I have a son who is 90." I like the sound of that, as long as my mother hasn't moved to Indiana to live with us. I would hate to have to kick my 50-year-old son out of his bedroom.

Most people love birthdays. They get excited at any mention of a date that is even remotely related to that special day. No matter whose day it is.

"Hey, Dick, when should we meet to discuss the new project?"

"How about April 7?"

"April 7? Wow! That's the day before my Uncle Sal's birthday!"

110

"Yeah, imagine that. How incredibly weird. I hope the whole day isn't going to be that spooky."

When I was a kid I loved birthdays. I've never been able to figure out why my attitude changed.

Of course, when I was eight years old I wasn't losing my hair, getting another chin, or walking around on one good knee. I wonder if that could have something to do with it? Nah.

Last week I received birthday cards from my financial advisor, my cardiologist, my lawyer, and my gardener. This troubles me. There are just so many hours in a day, and I would like to think people who work for me are spending their every free moment reading the latest professional journals, not looking for silly birthday cards.

As a result, I've hired a new cardiologist, financial advisor, and lawyer. But I'm sticking with my gardener. A man my age can only take so much change.

Hey, I'm almost 70.

36

MARK MY WORD

This has been a rough week for me. I have been abandoned by a woman I have depended on for many years. It is ironic that she should leave me just weeks before my Silver (silver?) wedding anniversary. The timing is particularly hurtful. My wife and I were headed for Germany to celebrate what I thought was 25 (twenty-five? twenty five?) years of marital bliss. The next thing I knew, my whole world turned inside out (inside-out?). Heidi jumped in (into?) a taxi cab (taxicab?) and headed to (for?) the airport.

Heidi is not my wife. Heidi is my proofreader (proof reader?). For the past five years, everything I've written has been sent to her via e-mail (email?) to make sure there are no mistakes.

Newspapers that publish my column do a great job of proofreading, but I wouldn't want whoever (whomever?) has that responsibility to think that on a day to day (day-to-day?) basis, I don't know what I'm doing. I would be really embarrassed if they continually (continuously?) found mistakes in my work.

Oh, I'm a pretty good speller and I even taught English for many years so I know my grammar, but when it comes to some of the other nuances of language, I'm a bit uptight (up tight? up-tight?). Gee, maybe I could reach Heidi over the internet (Internet?).

I think I'm a creative person, but I tend to be sloppier (more sloppy?) than I should be with the English language (Language?). Unless you have your own personal proofreader (proof reader?) like Heidi, you won't know if you're in the mood for an ice tea or an iced tea. Maybe some French fries (French Fries? french fries?). And when you get to the airport, you won't know whether (if?) you should check your carry-on luggage, carryon luggage, or carry on luggage.

A person like Heidi makes sure I am always consistent. In my new book about dogs, French poodles are always French poodles and never french poodles, or French Poodles. Yes, Heidi is always consistent. She may be consistently wrong, but at least she's consistent. That's the kind of person I can depend on (upon?). She may be the best proofer in the mid-west (Mid-West? midwest? Midwest?). Some writers would prefer a hands-off (hands off?) approach to their writing, but I really need help. I hope this has helped persuade (convince?) you.

I'm not implying (inferring?) that I couldn't do without her, but I think any disinterested (uninterested?) observer would admit that having your own copy editor (copyeditor?) is a slam dunk (slam-dunk?) decision.

When I first started writing my column about five years ago, I didn't really know the do's and don'ts (dos and don'ts?) of the language. I now know that a number of things is (are?) involved in writing perfect English. I've had discussions among (between?) a great number (amount?) of writers, and I know that they all agree that a person like Heidi gives credence (lends credibility?) to their work. Even if she sometimes squashes (quashes) your ego, she is the kind of person who (that?) every writer needs.

I can't wait until Heidi gets home. Every writer needs their (his, her) own proofreader. All I can say is that if you utilize (use?) someone like Heidi, you will be a lot (alot?) happier.

And my wife, Mary Ellen (Mary-Ellen?), agrees.

CHILD PROOF

This was the easiest newspaper column I have ever written. Why? Because I didn't write most of it. It was written by seventh grade students at Center Grove Middle School North in Greenwood, Indiana, inspired by their English teacher, Mrs. Gantz.

I take pride in coming up with new ideas for my daily TV segment and my weekly newspaper column. It's not easy—but no more difficult a task than it is for teachers who want to creatively challenge their students Monday through Friday. In August of 2006 I wrote a column about my proofreader, Heidi, who had taken a weeklong vacation to Hawaii and left me to fend for myself. Without Heidi I would be afraid to even use a word like fend, for fear it should have been feign. In my column, I pointed out to the reader (and to myself) all the fine points of language a proofreader (proof reader?) or copy editor (copyeditor?) must consider. Is it French Poodle or French poodle, or french poodle? Do you know? Are you sure?

When Mrs. Gantz saw my column in the local paper she seized what she called a "teaching moment." Passing out my column to her honors English class, she asked her students to form groups to research the correct answers. Not an easy assignment. Some proofreading issues are about style. There may not be a right or wrong answer, just a consistent usage that *The New York Times* prefers. Which may not be the way that *Sports Illustrated* does it. Or your local newspaper.

Of course, there are some clear right and wrong answers. The current standard is proofreader, not proof reader. No room for debate. You'll have to look up that poodle thing yourself.

Back to Mrs. Gantz's class. The students researched the answers. They could use a dictionary, a thesaurus, or the Internet. They then debated the issues among themselves. What a terrific project. I thought it was great. Heidi thought it was great. Mrs. Gantz thought it was great. But the kids? Well, part of the assignment was to write a letter to Heidi and me.

Here are some excerpts:

From this assignment, I learned proofreading is a real chore. I mean that in a bad way.

I did not like proofreading your column. If I have an offer to go to college and become a proofreader, I will definitely say no.

I think proofreading is a dreadful thing (Sorry, Heidi). I would rather just write the article.

Unless I got paid a lot of cash, I could never be a proofreader.

I think proofreading is a very boring job. Heidi must be a very brave person.

After much research I did come to one conclusion: I would never do this for a living.

I would call this an I-Want-to-Scratch-My-Eyeballs-Out kind of assignment.

I think that copyediting is about as much fun as washing windows.

In all fairness, many, many students loved the assignment and got a kick out of the research, praising Mrs. Gantz for her "neat idea." But this is a humor column, so I just shared the funny remarks. They gave me a good laugh.

This entire experience brought back memories of when I was a teacher. It was an awful long time ago. But I remember seizing a few "teaching opportunities" myself back in the '70s.

Your kids are lucky to have you, Mrs. Gantz. How cool it is to be a teacher. Thanks for reminding me what it felt like.

It was a Saturday morning and I was home alone. That had not happened to me once in 25 years, and I didn't know where to turn. Wherever I turned, there was no one there. I wasn't sure how to behave.

It all began when Brett and Mary Ellen attended a school activity in St. Louis. I was looking forward to a little time to myself, but I didn't realize how awkward I would feel. I'll never forget that Saturday morning.

Normally, I jump out of bed, knowing full well that before my wife and son manage to drag themselves out of a deep sleep, I can make myself what I want for breakfast, putter around the house, watch the Golf Channel, and write my newspaper column, all before the day officially begins and I get my "honey do list."

As usual, I awoke around five. Alone in the bed, alone in the house. Alone in the world. I felt incredibly ill-at-ease. What do I do now? I didn't have to get out of bed because I wasn't trying to beat anyone to the shower. I had no family errands to do. I had the whole day to goof off. But guess what? I wasn't sleepy. If this had been a workday, I'd have stayed in bed a bit longer, putting off the inevitable, but the problem here was: I DIDN'T HAVE TO GET UP! (It was okay to yell. No one was at home, remember?)

The dog was snoozing right next to me and could not relate to this dilemma. One of the great things about being a dog is that you seldom feel self-aware. Unless you're a French poodle.

So, did I get up? Well, I started to, and then I realized how many men get out of bed every morning either because they have to get up or they want to get up. And here I am with no real incentive to get up for any reason. I think there is a sociological term for this lack of ambition, and it applies to every extinct civilization. I'm no historian, but I am sure that at one point retired gladiators throughout ancient Rome were waking up and saying, "I don't really have to get up, so why the heck should I?"

I finally hobbled downstairs and made myself a cup of coffee and a bowl of cereal. I made a mess in the kitchen, spilled coffee grounds all over the counter, and used my hand to wipe my mouth when I couldn't find a napkin. Then I left the kitchen in a total mess and went into the living room and watched the Golf Channel for an hour in my underwear with the volume turned up really loud. I even opened a bottle of beer. I couldn't bear to drink it at 6 a.m., but I wanted to prove how much potential I had as a free spirit.

This would usually be about the time my wife would come downstairs and tell me to clean up my mess, turn off the TV, put on some clothes, and clean the garage. I have to admit, I actually missed that. It made me realize how much I love my family. It made me feel empty the whole day.

Some days it just doesn't pay to get out of bed.

HORSING AROUND

Because the Colts were not in the Super Bowl in 2006, I did not want to waste three solid hours watching the annual extravaganza. Instead, I decided to write my column while watching the game, taking a writing break only during the really exciting parts, like the commercials or the artistic shots of the cheerleaders. My wife said this was a stupid idea and that if I was distracted while working, the column would be really, really bad.

As I readied myself with chips, salsa, and mini egg rolls, an article in the newspaper caught my eye. Apparently, South Dakota, of all places, has bested us again in the area of legislative innovation. A new law in the Mount Rushmore State basically says that while the authorities will throw you in the slammer for driving your Chevy pick-up after downing six pints of hard lemonades, it is now perfectly legal to ride your bike down Main Street even after enjoying several Bloody Marys.

And, in an attachment to the bill, it is also now legal in South Dakota to get completely looped as long as you ride home on your mustang and not in your Mustang. Let me translate all this: You can be drunk on your horse or on your bike but not in your car.

Why have Indiana lawmakers been wasting their time arguing about abortion, Ten Commandments, I-69, I-STEP, and the cigarette tax, while more progressive states have figured out the kind of legislative action that really makes a difference to the average citizen?

I hope they pass a law like this in Indiana because I can't tell you how many times I've had a few too many over at my local watering hole then driven home, instead of getting my Clydesdale out of the backseat of my Hyundai and trotting my drunk rear-end back to my house.

In South Dakota, this law was not without its critics. Lots of Dakotans claimed that many locals actually drink with their horses and while some of the steeds can hold their liquor, many of the less sophisticated breeds—like Pintos—get wrecked (so to speak) on one glass of Merlot. If you're driving behind a Pinto, be verrrry careful. Heh, heh.

According to lawmakers who championed the bill, there have been a few setbacks. In one case, a rider who was apparently drunk caused a four-car pile-

up by galloping his horse through a red light. After a breathalyzer test, it was determined that the rider was stone sober. But the horse was crocked. The horse refused the breathalyzer test and had to appear in court. The horse's lawyer claimed that the bartender who gave his client the fifth glass of ChardonNAY should also be held responsible. The bartender said it was hard for him to turn down a customer with such a long face, which shows that while wine may get better with age, some jokes remain just as bad.

Well, the Super Bowl just ended. After reading this you may question whether it's a good idea to try to write an essay and pay attention to a sporting event at the same time. Look at the bright side: If the Colts had been in the Super Bowl, this column would have been even more lame.

40

CRAMPING MY STYLE

↑ ↓

I have leg cramps. I know the last thing you want to hear about are the medical problems of some two-bit humorist.

Actually, I've been surprised lately at how many people really do care about the fact that my calf locks up in a knot at night and the pain is so unbearable I feel like I'm giving birth to a Volkswagen.

When you're as old as I am, I think it's better to only have friends in your own age group. If I told a 30-year-old guy I had leg cramps, or shortness of breath, or was thinking of asking the doctor for those little blue pills, he'd just shake his head, put the iPod in his ear, jump in his Mini Cooper and take off.

Recently I was in an elevator and a young man who had been a recent intern at WISH-TV was chatting with me.

"So how have you been, Mr. Wolfsie?"

"Oh, okay I guess, Todd, but I do get these terrible leg cramps at night."

"Well, have a nice day. See ya."

On the way down in the elevator, I saw an old friend—a man of my own vintage.

"Hey, Dick, how ya doin'?"

"Fine, Joel, except at night I do get these leg…"

"Don't tell me…leg cramps. I used to get them, too. Here's what I recommend: Take vitamin E three times a day. It's like a miracle."

I've never trusted the Internet for health information, but I am inclined to take advice in an elevator. To be sure, I did call my doctor to ask his opinion. He told me that vitamin E was not good for me because of an interaction with other medication I am taking for my cholesterol. Then he asked me exactly where I had gotten this faulty information. I told him the 14th floor of the building we were in. That's all he needs to know.

The next day, back on that same elevator, I ran into another old buddy—"old" being the key word here, again.

"Hey, Dick, word is out you are having leg cramps."

"Wow, word sure travels up and down fast in this building."

"My dad had leg cramps and he drank a gin and tonic every night for 30 years before he went to bed—and he never had cramps again."

"What did it? The gin or the tonic?"

"Who cares? It worked."

I did some Googling and found that the gin helps you forget your pain, but it was probably the quinine in the tonic that really eased the cramps. For the next two weeks, I drank a quart of tonic before bed. It had little effect on the problem, so now I'm willing to at least consider the therapeutic benefit of gin.

Over the course of the month, I asked several friends, a few doctors, and even my good buddy Wendell Fowler, the nutritionist guru in Indy, about any possible remedies for my ailment. Here, in no particular order, are the cures that people swear by.

Magnesium

Zinc

Vitamin E

Turmeric

Potassium

Vitamin C

Acupuncture

Biofeedback

Folic acid

Calcium

Fiber pills

Cauliflower extract

Yoga

I am not going to take any of this advice, but I have noticed lately that my legs do tend to cramp at night on days when I have vigorously ridden my exercise bike. I'm no doctor, but I am prescribing to myself a complete lack of physical activity for the next six months and a shot of gin before going to bed.

I'd take it with tonic water, but I don't believe everything I hear in elevators.

41

SOAP DUDS

I always get a smattering of e-mails after I write a column. Newspaper writers know that most of their stuff ends up in the garbage along with the moldy cheese or in the recycle bin, assuming the reader is environmentally friendly. So it is always a real kick to learn that someone has cut out my column and stuck it up on the refrigerator next to their first grader's finger-painting or under a Rachel Ray recipe for chicken fricassee. That's about the most I could ask for.

But the piece I wrote a few weeks ago about my legs cramps resulted in the most e-mails I'd ever gotten in response to one of my columns. I would tell you how many e-mails there were, but I'd rather you had an image of my computer service calling to tell me that I'd overloaded the system and that I can't publish any more humor columns that touch the very fabric and nerve of the reading public.

The story was about my nighttime leg cramps. In the column I complained about this persistent problem, and mentioned that I had gotten a great deal of advice from people who also suffered from this malady. Here were a few of the suggestions, just to refresh your memory:

Magnesium, Zinc, Vitamin E, Turmeric, Potassium, Vitamin C, Acupuncture, Biofeedback Folic acid, Calcium. Quinine, Fiber pills Cauliflower extract, Yoga, Black cherry extract.

After the column appeared, I started getting e-mails that began like this:

"Dick, ever think of using soap?"

"Mr. Wolfsie, do you realize the importance of a bar of soap?"

"Hey, DW, a bar of soap can make a big difference in your life."

At first, I was mortified. I'm not a hygiene fanatic, but I don't think I missed a shower all last year— except that one morning I had to rush the dog to the vet when he swallowed an AAA Alkaline battery. I *was* a little sweaty in the waiting room, but if people are going to take a whiff of you during a crisis they shouldn't be judgmental.

All the e-mails contained a similar suggestion: to cure leg cramps sleep with a bar of soap in your bed. I was a bit cautious, of course. Maybe it was a grand conspiracy to tantalize me to do something really bizarre; then they could all laugh themselves silly about Dick Wolfsie at the office Christmas party, just at the mere prospect I may have fallen for it.

I showed these e-mails to my doctor that week. He said that he often recommended putting a bar of soap in the bed but hadn't mentioned it to me because he figured I already knew about it. Now, how would I know to put a bar of soap in my bed to cure cramps? Did I go to medical school like he did?

Anyway, that evening I tried it. I was just hoping Mary Ellen wouldn't notice, because she's always accusing me of falling for every wacky idea out there.

"Dick, what's that strong soapy smell?

"Look, Mary Ellen, please don't think I'm totally nuts. And please don't think I'll believe every off-the-wall suggestion that people e-mail me, but that odor is actually a bar of Dial soap that I placed in between the sheets of the bed."

"Well, I don't know why you'd do something so incredibly weird like that, but look at the bright side, at least it might cure those leg cramps."

42

HOT DOG

The state legislature in Florida is considering a bill that would permit dogs to accompany their owners to restaurants with outdoor seating. This is really far bigger news to dogs than it is to humans.

What's interesting about this is that no one has asked dogs what they think of the idea. In Boca, many Pekingese never see a newspaper. Most Cockers have no Internet access. Beagles get most of their news from Fox, and there's little information to help the average working dog.

Nonetheless, dogs and man can now dine together. But do dogs care? Just imagine: All curled up on the sofa, snoozing away on a lazy evening, and all of a sudden you are grabbed by the scruff of your neck and forced to go out for dinner. I hate it when

Mary Ellen does that to me, so imagine how an Irish Setter would feel.

A Jack Russell with any bounce left in him will tell you that the last thing he wants to do is lie around a crowded restaurant waiting for the unlikely chance that some waitress will knock a chunk of beef tenderloin off the plate for the real meat-lover in the family. Suppose you're a Chihuahua and it's a hot day—just try to get the waitress's attention for a bowl of water. Good luck.

Truth is that to most dogs the enactment of such legislation will prove to be nothing but frustration at every curb. Biscuits and gravy may sound appetizing to the average pooch, but the pale mushy breakfast fare will be a disappointment to the dog who envisioned sinking his teeth into a crunchy treat covered with beefy sauce.

Of course, some canines will get a taste of the good life and want to go solo to their favorite eateries. Acquiring a credit card is not a problem for working dogs like Border Collies, but a low-life poodle with no prospect of employment will never be able to get a Visa. Although, I do have a friend who swears that Master Card sent her Siamese cat a credit card.

There is already resistance from people, as well—people who claim they are allergic to dogs and that one whiff of a Rottweiler puts them in anaphylactic shock and gives them a rash the size of a '78 Buick. No doubt these are the same incessant complainers who won't share an elevator with a gentleman puffing an aromatic Cuban cigar. Whiners!

Of course, this is all about big money for the restaurateurs who know that no dog owner would order something for himself without at least glancing at the new doggie menu. At Starbucks a bowl of Aqua Latte would sell for $2.75 and Espresso Rawhide for $4.00. Bones and Scones, $7.50.

I hope they pass an ordinance in Indy allowing you to bring your dog to a restaurant. Then, I'd like to see a sign that said:

NO CATS ALLOWED

Dogs have been the victims of discrimination for too long in this country.

FUNNY YOU SHOULD SAY THAT

Do you think this is easy? Seriously. Do you think it's easy coming up with something funny every week for a newspaper column?

Right now, you're probably saying one of three things:

- Hey, who's he kidding? I read his stuff all the time. He doesn't come up with something funny every week.

- Oh, this is supposed to be humorous?

- I don't think it would be that hard. I wish I had a newspaper column.

Abracadabra... now you do!. OK, wise guy (or girl), what are you going to write about? Better hurry. Your deadline is in four hours.

I really hope you'll consider this opportunity because right now, as I look back on the past week, my life has been pretty uneventful. No good material to work with.

Let's see, I did lose my appointment book and finally found it in the freezer. I had it in my hand when I went to get ice cream, and I left it in there. Now the pages of June, July, and August are all frozen together. Nada, nothing funny there.

I went shopping the other day at Sam's Club, and when I came out to the parking lot, I looked for my tan Suzuki for more than an hour. After I called the police to report it stolen, I realized I had driven my wife's green Toyota Camry. No. Nobody would find that funny.

I lost my cell phone again. I had set it down in the bottom of a large container while I opened a bag of dog food. Then I dumped the dog food on top of the phone and covered it up. For three days, the dog food was ringing. That's not even worth a giggle.

I went to school to talk to my son's English teacher to discuss a problem, and I was a little put off that after four months she didn't have a really good idea of who my son was. Of course, I was talking to the wrong teacher. Nuts. No one will find that humorous.

OK, how's this? My beagle, Toby, jumped in the backseat of the plumber's car and fell asleep while it was parked in the driveway. The plumber went home with him in the car, and I had to drive 40 miles to get the dog. That won't work. No one is going to laugh at that.

Let's see. I paid some tech geek $60 to come to my house just to tell me that the computer's plug had come out of the wall. No, nothing there.

I bought my wife a very sexy number at Victoria's Secret, but they had to order it out of the catalog. I was a little distracted, so I gave them my old home address by mistake, and now I have to tell my 87-year-old mother that the black lace teddy is not for her. Darn, that won't work either.

I renewed my subscription to *USA Today* through their website, but I must have clicked something wrong because they have been leaving me 25 copies every morning on my doorstep, and I can't get them to stop. Nope, that's not funny.

I posted my latest book on eBay to sell for $10 per copy, but it was posted as 10 cents by mistake, and still nobody bought one.

That's definitely not funny.

44

I DARE YOU

I'm one of those men who really enjoys a good challenge. I once took four naps in one day, breaking an old family record. I've watched football for 13 straight hours on TV, and I went a whole week (this was in college, I swear) wearing the same underwear. I am no stranger to competition.

Last week my friend Bob said to me over lunch, "Can you write a humor column about anything?"

"Of course," I bragged. "A good humorist does not require an offbeat topic. I can take any common, everyday event and successfully write something funny."

I don't know what made me say something so incredibly stupid, but when the waitress brought me my sixth Bud Light, Bob took the opportunity to put me to the test.

"I know you listen to books on tape. Write something funny about that. I dare you."

I tried to wiggle out of it, but after downing a few beers, I knew I couldn't win a debate with a man sipping club soda.

Okay, here goes. Just remember, this wasn't my idea.

AUTO EROTIC

I'm not a very good driver. I once swerved to avoid hitting an evergreen tree, and it was my car's air freshener hanging on the rearview mirror.

That's why my wife is a little concerned when I listen to books on tape in the car. She thinks that if I'm driving and someone is talking, I may not pay attention to what I am doing. The theory has a few holes in it because in 25 years of taxiing my wife to all our social obligations, I have successfully screened out just about every household chore Mary Ellen has reminded me to do while she was sitting in the passenger seat yakking away. Don't tell me I can't focus on driving.

On the other hand, I am sometimes too easily lost in thought, which can be dangerous. The other day I was listening to a tape on the history of Old English from Geoffrey Chaucer to William Shakespeare, a classic example of the type of intellectual stimulation that I prefer while motoring around the Midwest. I was on my way from Indy to Kokomo, and long about the 15th century, I started thinking about Sharon Stone in *Basic Instinct*. The next thing I knew I was in a Detroit suburb.

My wife thinks my obsession with "reading" in the car has gone too far.

"It's one thing listening to tapes during the day, but now you're listening to them at night. I'm having trouble sleeping."

"You can hear the tape?"

"No, but I worry about you in the car with the motor on and the garage door closed."

Recently, I convinced my wife to get a few of her favorite novels on tape so she could listen in the car, also.

"I must admit, Dick, this is very entertaining, very engrossing. But, unlike you, I am able to do two things at once. By the way, you need to make a left at the next stop sign."

"I would, Mary Ellen but you're the one who's driving."

(This is a cheap ending, I know, but at least I won the bet when I said I could write a funny article about anything.)

I did win, didn't I?

45

TAKE THIS JOB AND LOVE IT

Several years ago some nutty company came out with the 10 best jobs in America. By best, they apparently meant the most money with the least stress. As I reported then, their number one pick was biologist. But the results you get on a survey like this depend on who picks up the phone. The biologist at Edy's Ice Cream would probably have a different take on life than the biologist at the National Institutes of Health who is juggling vials of Avian Flu.

This same survey also listed the most stressful jobs, such as lumberjack. Lumberjack? At the time, I had never met an unhappy lumberjack. What's not to be happy about? You're outdoors, you're exercising, there are no meetings. You can wear the same shirt every day. The truth is, I have never met a lumberjack socially, although one once nearly hit me with an axe at the Indianapolis Boat, Sport and Travel Show three years ago. I don't think being a lumberjack is stressful. Okay, there's no casual Friday, but I think most lumberjacks are pretty laid back. They let the chips fall where they may.

The job with the highest stress was President of the United States. Why? There is no job security, and it pays about 90 percent less than a pro basketball player makes. This is why only about six people vie for the job every four years. Maybe if we increased the pay and threw in a few 'get out of jail free' cards, it would be more popular. Clinton found some nifty ways to relieve stress, but George Bush claims he's never made a mistake, which does put a lot of pressure on Dubya to keep his perfect record.

Another high-stress job was race car driver. I once rode as a passenger in a car like this, and when you are going speeds in excess of 160 miles per hour and making sharp turns, it's nerve-racking. Plus the driver spoke no English, which frightened me even more.

Also on the list was New York City cab driver. I once rode as a passenger in a car like this, and when you are going speeds in excess of 160 miles per hour and making sharp turns, it's nerve-racking. Plus the driver spoke no English, which frightened me even more.

NFL football player was on one of the lists. That is a stressful job, and who wants to work on Sundays? I think these guys need a better union.

School teacher was on the list. The inner city school environment can be stressful. Years ago, I remember my mother telling me one morning that I needed to put my fears aside, ignore the fact that I wasn't getting along with most of the kids, and try to make a better impression on the teachers. I was the assistant principal at the time.

Customer service specialist also made the list. They listen to complaints. Many of these folks were turned down as Yellow Shirts at the Indianapolis Motor Speedway because they were even too unpleasant for that job.

Anyway, lists like these are on my list of things that annoy me. Reading lists stresses me out. As I've noted before, I prefer to be listless.

LAUGH LINES

My wife, Mary Ellen, is a warm, caring, sensitive human being. So when I turned to her the other night at dinner and said, "I don't think there's anything funny left to write about—I may have to discontinue my humor column," I wasn't surprised when she replied, "Pass the salt."

I am suffering from writer's block. I've written about it before. Writer's block is when, well it's kind of like, you know, it happens after you…it's a time when you can't…I think you get the picture.

I first knew I had it several weeks ago when I awoke in the middle of the night sweating, with my heart palpitating and discomfort in my chest. At first, I thought it was a heart attack. With a heart attack, trained physicians can put you on a table, insert a tube in your leg, and then shove it into your groin and up to your heart to clear the blockage. I should be so lucky. At least there's a treatment.

Mary Ellen takes my sense of humor for granted. Many wives assume their husbands will be polite and courteous at all times. Other wives assume their husbands will be sincere and caring. Mary Ellen jumps to no such conclusions.

Instead, she assumes that when our waitress comes over to the table sporting a pierced tongue, lavender-colored hair, and stiletto army boots, that I'll say something humorous—something that strikes the perfect note, making fun of our server but not humiliating or embarrassing her. I admit it's a gift, but I'd still like a bit more understanding from my wife about the writer's block.

"Why aren't you more sympathetic to my problem, Mary Ellen?"

"You don't have a humor block, Dick. You say this every few months. Look, I'll prove it. If I asked you, 'Why did you go to Taco Bell yesterday and eat three burritos for breakfast?' what would you say?"

"Let's see...I'd probably say that I wanted to go somewhere I could get gas for under three dollars."

"See? You're still on your game. Suppose I said that I wanted you to enjoy a wonderful dinner tonight, so what should I make? What would you say?"

"Reservations."

"See, you're fine. You haven't lost it. Suppose I suggested that you needed more confidence in the romance department. What would you say?"

"I'd say that's ridiculous, but when we kiss I do fantasize that I'm somebody else."

"Dick, that was great. I almost cracked a smile. Now, one more straight line. How expensive are gas prices?"

"Pretty bad. This year it may have to be the Indianapolis 200."

"I rest my case. You're still hot."

"Wait a second, those are punch lines I stole from Henny Youngman, Conan O'Brien, Richard Lewis, and Jay Leno."

"Dick, let's be realistic. You're not Jerry Seinfeld, you're Dick Wolfsie. Work with what you have."

She was right. Maybe my expectations are too high. I can't come up with an idea for a column every week and expect each one to be hysterical. Sometimes I just have to hand in a piece that's mediocre and hope that nobody will really notice.

Did you?

47

PHOTOGRAPHIC MEMORIES

I am a loser. I lose everything. Most people lose golf balls on a course; I lose clubs. People lose their wallets; I lose my pants. Don't ask. It's a long story.

Once after I had lost my keys for the third time in a week, my wife found them in two minutes. "How did you do that so quickly?" I asked.

"It's real simple, Dick. You don't look very good."

"You need to rephrase that, Mary Ellen. My ego is already bruised."

"Let's say you don't look well."

"So I need a doctor?"

"You're twisting my words. You're a loser. Just accept it."

"I should have quit when I needed a doctor."

The truth is I am not very focused, which brings me to my latest mishap in being careless with my stuff.

On our family vacation to Montreal in 2006, I put my digital camera in the little plastic box to go through the scanner at the airport. Then I forgot to retrieve it when it exited the conveyor. When I came back five minutes later, it was gone.

The camera was chock-full of pictures showing all the fun Mary Ellen, Brett (my son), and I had— you know, standing in front of an old church, standing in front of an old restaurant, standing in front of an old museum, standing in front of old people.

At this point I want to thank those complete strangers in Canada who were willing to take photos of us. The photo I really wanted to see was taken when Mary Ellen and Brett went on a roller coaster, and I stayed behind and asked this guy if he would snap a photo of me with his gorgeous girlfriend.

But back to my loss: I was hoping the thief might have had some change of heart about taking my camera. I did have my name and e-mail address taped on the back. Hey, even crooks can have a conscience. But this guy in Montreal takes the cake...I mean the Kodak.

Last week I opened up my e-mail and there was this note:

Dear Mr. Wolfsie:

Thanks for leaving your camera unattended at the Montreal airport. I've always wanted one like that. But when I started looking through those pictures, my heart just went out to you. You have such a lovely family, so I am e-mailing you all your photos.

But now, just a few suggestions from an objective observer. Your wife is very attractive, but tell her to lose the capri pants. Not flattering to her figure. And what's with you and the white socks with sandals? And tell your son not to slouch. Here's a thought: How about some more candid shots of the family actually doing something instead of all those posed photos? Geez, have some fun. The Wolfsies look very stiff.

Anyway, Dick, if I may call you that (after all, I feel like I know your whole family), I am keeping the camera, even though I would have preferred a Nikon. Some final advice: I know you probably think half a head is better than none. Not in photography.

I hope you take this advice—it cost you about $500.00.

P.S. Do you know if they make a carrying case for that camera? Also, could I have the phone number of that blonde with you in front of the roller coaster?

48

LIAR
LIAR
LIAR

I'm a liar. A no-good, rotten liar. I used to be comfortable with my digressions from the truth. But now I'm ashamed to have sunk this low. This is what happens when you become a writer.

Normally, I wouldn't care that much. A person who lies doesn't usually feel real guilty about it—that's who he is and he is just being honest with himself. Of course, he could lie to himself, but he knows who he is and he's the last person in the world he's going to believe.

This all started last week when I wrote a newspaper column about how I went on a vacation with my family to Canada. That was true. Then how I put my digital camera through the security scanner. Totally factual. And how it was stolen when I left it behind. Correct, again.

I wanted to write about this incident. And I had the best intentions of telling a story about how careless I am with my things. But when I got back to work the day after our trip, I ran into Joy Dumandan, the morning co-anchor at WISH-TV…

"How was your vacation, Dick?" she asked.

"Oh, it was great. Except my camera was stolen."

"What a shame." And with all your photos."

"It's okay—the thief e-mailed me the pictures."

I don't know where that came from. It just slid out of my mouth. It wasn't just an exaggeration, it was a bold-faced fabrication.

With that, Joy got hysterical laughing; she couldn't stop.

"Hey, Joy, I was only…I was only kidd…

Before I got the word out, she had told Dave Barras, the other morning anchor at the time. Then Dave started laughing….

"Dave, as I tried to tell Joy, I was just kidd…kidd…I mean it was probably just some kid who needed a camera."

The word spread. I was the talk of the station. "I hear you have a very funny vacation story," people said to me. All day long I repeated the incident, so when I sat down that night to write my column, I was starting to believe the whole thing myself. When you repeat something enough times, you start thinking it's the truth. Just ask the (fill in your political party of choice).

In my column, I even included a bogus e-mail from the thief who stole my camera. I had already entered the dark side—why not get a few laughs in the process?

Dear Mr. Wolfsie:

Thanks for leaving your camera unattended at the Montreal airport. I've always wanted one like that. But when I started looking through those pictures, my heart just went out to you. You have such a lovely family, so I am e-mailing you all your photos.

After the column was published, I received dozens of e-mails.

Dear Dick,

Your column was hysterical. You took a real-life negative experience and let us laugh at your expense.

• • •

Dear Dick,

Very funny column. This could only happen to you. Great stuff.

• • •

Witty as always, Dick. We love the honesty in your writing.

The guilt was killing me. I just hope the person who stole my camera reads this column and has the decency to e-mail me my pictures.

I don't care about the stupid photos; I just want to be an honest man again.

49

According to *Good Morning America*, there's a new reality show in England that has all the women talking. It's actually the husbands, however, who are yapping about this. I better explain.

The program is called *Bring Your Husband to Heel*, and the creator of this show claims you can use the very same principles to teach your husband to behave as you do to teach your Lhasa Apso or your Shih Tzu.

It is important that you realize we are talking specifically about dogs, not pets in general. Husbands are already like cats. They pay no attention to you, sleep all day, and are always on the wrong side of the door. The big difference is that men don't mind a dirty litter box and, unlike a cat, if you don't clean a man's bathroom, he'll still use it for close to a decade. Husbands are, however, often like skunks and snakes. Or so I have heard.

The woman who is hosting the show asserts her results are undeniable and that she has trained her husband to be the perfect mate. "Since I started using dog-training techniques, I have not had to wash a single dish," she said. Yes, It's great to have clean dishes, but her husband's tongue has been badly damaged by all the plate licking. And his back and knees are just killing him.

Sadly, my wife got a hold of some information concerning the show and has been trying out a few sure-fire techniques. When I noticed her experimenting with some of these methods, I told her I wasn't going to take it lying down, which sounded kind of stupid since I had just rolled over and played dead so I could have another beer.

The whole thing began to get out of hand so I tried to give her a little scare. After dinner, for example, we usually stroll around the lake in our neighborhood. When she said, "Dick, do you want to go for a walk?" I made my backside rotate in anticipation.

"You're not taking this seriously, Dick. I am simply applying basic behavioral techniques to our relationship, and you are making a mockery of it."

"You don't think it's funny when I get out of the shower and shake instead of towel off?"

"Yes, that's cute, but driving with your head sticking out the window is dangerous. And when

 you come home from work, please just use your key. The scratching at the front door is driving me crazy."

Of course, there were some advantages to this experiment. I got more belly rubs in one week than I got in the previous 25 years of marriage. I am allowed to "go out" as often as I want, but that electric collar is really cramping my style. The spay/neuter brochure that Mary Ellen picked up at the vet put me a little on edge.

I was still expected to do normal husband stuff. Mary Ellen sent me out to fetch…I mean pick up items at the store. Although, at the bottom of a long list of things to get at Marsh, she wrote, "While you are out, why don't you get a bath."

This silliness had gone on long enough. I didn't want my wife to treat me like a dog any more. So last weekend I took her out for a very elegant dinner and bought her roses and champagne. I was looking forward to a very romantic evening when we got home.

She told me to get off the bed.

50

SNAP CRACKLE POP

Hold on to your Sugar Pops and listen to this: I read in *The New York Times* the other day that the hottest new dietary fad among college kids is cereal. Yes, cereal—like Rice Krispies, Corn Flakes, Cocoa Puffs and, for those with a military bent, Cap'n Crunch.

While the parents of these college kids are feeling wobbly and light-headed from the Atkins diet, college campuses like the University of Pennsylvania are seeing a trend in new restaurants that actually serve nothing but cereal. Mom and Dad are sitting down to a 10-ounce rib-eye steak at the club while their daughter Kimberly is at U of P scarfing down 10 ounces of Honey Nut Cheerios.

When I was a kid in the '50s, you had three choices for breakfast: Shredded Wheat, Rice Krispies, or

Corn Flakes. Some parents in the '50s chose bacon and eggs every morning for their children. May they all rest in peace.

People say nowadays that life is complicated for adolescents; what with drugs and sex and violent video games, the average 15-year-old is surrounded by temptation. With 176 different cereals on the shelves (the people at Marsh thought I was a cereal stalker), kids don't know which way to turn.

I remember what I went through when Froot Loops and Cocoa Puffs both hit the shelves about the same time. At 17, my hormones were already kicking into gear, and this convenient sugar buzz threw my entire endocrine system out of whack. Here were cereals already sweetened. What an enticement to eat them right out of the box! Where was the Religious Right when you needed them?

Then Trix made a big splash, and these little multi-colored sugar nuggets with their alluring shapes had cult written all over them. Kids in my elementary school were stuffing them in their pockets and eating them during class and in the halls. Teachers had to sneak theirs in the rest-room stalls because, alas, Trix were for kids.

By the way, Shredded Wheat was always problematic to me. Here was a cereal that never had a good working relationship with milk. The milk either rolled off it and the

Shredded Wheat remained dry, or if you had the wherewithal to push the cereal down into the milk with your fist (they were surprisingly buoyant), the Shredded Wheat ended up soggy. Shredded Wheat never mastered consummate moistureness like Frosted Flakes did.

A team of Ph.D.s at Post decided that instead of letting you put succulent fruit on top of cereal yourself, they would take bananas, blueberries, and strawberries, freeze-dry them, and put them in the cereal box for you. These are the same people who named a cereal "Grape-Nuts," a product with no nuts and no grapes. HUH?

As a kid I'd jam my hand down into the cereal box and span out my fingers in search of the Secret Decoder Ring. That quest was the high point of my morning. They don't put stuff like that in cereal boxes anymore because people were swallowing their decoder rings and Kellogg's had to replace all the Ph.D.s with attorneys.

Even at 60, if I had a choice to have a decoder ring or a freeze-dried strawberry in my cereal box, I think you know which one I'd pick.

51

ICE PRINCESS

Most of the wives in my neighborhood will do something for their husbands that Mary Ellen won't do. Maybe it was her upbringing. Maybe she just gets cold feet.

She won't shovel snow.

I walked out on my front porch to get the newspaper the morning after the storm that pelted central Indiana the week of Christmas 2005. Sure enough, there were Julie, Angie, Kelly, and Nancy out there pushing the snow shovel, clearing their driveways, and having so much fun. I grabbed my shovel and joined in the party.

"Are you doing OK?" screamed Julie. "Where's Mary Ellen?"

"Oh, she's in the house probably cleaning the chimney or painting our crawl space. It's my turn to shovel snow."

Where was Mary Ellen? She was in our warm, toasty kitchen, that's where she was. I couldn't stand it anymore. I was so angry, I stormed into the house. But not before I dusted the snow off my gloves, took off my wet boots, and hung my damp coat up in the bathroom. I didn't want to tick her off before I gave her a piece of my mind.

"Mary Ellen, did you know that I'm out there shoveling snow and I have a minor heart condition?"

"I know that, Dick. How selfish are you? While you're out there playing in the snow, gossiping with all the neighborhood women, I'm inside this hot kitchen trying to find a low-fat holiday recipe to meet your sausage obsession."

I never did ask her why she won't shovel. I was afraid she'd assume it was important to me. This couldn't be farther from the truth. If she started shoveling snow, that would jeopardize our relationship by altering the delicate balance between my wife's independence and her femininity.

Of course, if she really wanted to shovel snow, I wouldn't stop her.

When I decided to marry Mary Ellen, I guess it didn't matter. I mean, after all, she was intelligent, beautiful, sensitive, and caring. It was all a man could want. I guess I just assumed that if push came to shove, she'd shovel snow. And I bet if I had a really bad back problem and the snow was really deep, she would shovel, then.

Sometimes I watch those other women shoveling and I actually find it kind of unattractive. I mean, they're wearing layers of old ratty sweat pants and big puffy coats and work boots. Of course, I wouldn't have to watch. And if Mary Ellen did shovel, she could just freshen up and join me in front of the fire.

I actually think it's kind of chauvinistic for a man to make his wife shovel snow. Of course, on the other hand, it's kind of chauvinistic for a man to assume that a woman can't or won't shovel snow, so I guess I should at least ask her.

Maybe she really wants to shovel snow but is afraid I won't let her. I'm sure that's it.

I'd even buy her a snow blower, just to show her I care and that I'm behind her 100 percent. But who am I kidding? Mary Ellen won't do snow.

What's wrong with her, anyway? My friend, Jeff, his wife shovels snow. He was over the other day and asked me why Mary Ellen never shovels snow. I was as honest with him as I could be.

"I don't know, Jeff. I never really thought about it."

52

SORRY WRONG NUMBER

The wonderful people who bring you the SATs announced that they made a mathematical mistake when they corrected some of the exams this past academic year and that some students received scores 100 points lower than they should have. Maybe 120. But who's counting?

Apparently no one who really knows how to do math.

The College Board people who administer the exam said it was nothing to be alarmed about. At first, they just said they made some technical errors. Hey, that's exactly what I told my parents when I got a 280 on the math exam in 1963. Then came the official reason from the Board: *Moisture caused the answer sheets to expand before they were scanned.* Man, that is a great excuse. Why didn't I think of that one when I was a kid?

The Board went on to say that it only affected .08 percent of the 495,000 students who took the test. When asked how many people that was in actual numbers, they said they weren't really sure.

These are the same people who would ask an innocent child something like:

If $x(-3) = 64$, what is the value of $X/1.8$?

They can't wait to start deducting points to keep the masses out of Yale or Harvard, then they turn around and can't add up a poor kid's score to within a hundred points. Shame!

Then, to make matters worse, we get questions like this:

> The cells of a bacteria colony grow by each splitting into two cells every two hours. If after 18 hours from the start of an experiment, the colony grows to the square root of 5.7, how many cells were in the colony when the experiment began?

I have no idea what the answer is to this question. I think what's important is that someone needs to get into that lab and stop all that multiplying. If those were people doing all that multiplying, we'd send in a commission or some religious leaders. Not only that but turning the whole thing into a math problem kind of takes all the romance out of reproducing.

I sometimes wonder if they messed up my score 45 years ago when I took my SATs. It would kill me to know that I've been walking around for the last four decades under the misconception that glove is to hand as hat is to head. Maybe B was correct: Hand is to glove as banana is to pocket. Being a big fruit lover, it would have garnered me a lot of Mae West jokes.

And the more I think about it, the more frustrated I get. I remember one question from my test that went something like this:

> A train leaves the station going 150 mph. You leave your home on your bike going 12 mph. If you started 200 miles apart, when would you and the train meet?

That question really gave me nightmares—and I walked to school for the next two months. I originally thought I got that one right, but now as an adult I seem to always be late for trains…so maybe the Board screwed up that question, too.

The College Board said they plan to return all the registration fees to the .08 percent of the 495,000 students who were affected by this.

Let's see, that's a $41.50 registration fee times .08 percent of 495,000 plus .08 percent of 495,000 for stamps at 39 cents each, which comes to somewhere in the neighborhood of:

a) $72,284.87

b) $123,003.98

c) $23.46

d) A lot, give or take 100 or so

e) All of the above

53

WRONGFUL BIRTH

Sometimes I wonder if 1947 was the wrong year to be born.

Some really cool things *did* happen in 1947. Jackie Robinson was named Rookie of the Year and Howdy Doody debuted on TV. I was too young to realize how earth-shattering those two events would be, but I'm proud to have been part of the very same year.

By the way, on a complete list of other great things that happened in 1947, my birth is not to be found. And I checked the list several times. The list *does* include things like:

- Goodrich announced the development of the tubeless tire in Akron.

- The tennis shoe was introduced.

I'm not complaining—just wondering how these list makers can earn any respect when they come up with twaddle like that and ignore my birth altogether.

Truth is, I sometimes wish I had just been born a few months earlier; it could have had a profound effect on my life.

For example, it was only six weeks after I left my fledgling baseball career behind me as a young adolescent that some genius finally realized that Little League uniforms should not be made of wool, and that a lot of the passing out while running around the bases in those days was linked to having a body temperature of 200 degrees in your tweed pants.

Here's another example: If my calculations are correct, I graduated from college in 1968 and missed the sexual revolution by about a month, which doesn't seem so bad except it sure would have made that last four weeks of school a little more memorable.

Now an article in the newspaper the other day has really put me over the edge. Maybe I was born 54 years too *late*. Apparently, pediatricians are now saying that if your mother raised you with a diet of bland cereal and mashed peas, she was doing you a disservice. The newest research recommends spicier foods like enchiladas. Even an occasional hot pepper. There is no doubt that these are the conclusions of male researchers who do not have to change diapers.

I can tell you right now that my mother never gave me an enchilada when I was an infant. I don't have a clear memory of being fed when I was that young, but your body doesn't lie and I still gag when I walk down the baby food aisle on the way to the Budweiser display.

You have to wonder who decided to do this research…

"Hey, Dr. Barnes, how's your research going?"

"I'm studying the effects of air pollutants on infants who live in urban areas. But I'm bored to death. Who cares about this stuff, anyway?"

"Got any better ideas?"

"Ever wonder what the effect on infants would be if instead of Gerber Baby Peaches you gave them a Burrito Grande or a Taco Supreme for dinner? That's research you can sink your gums into."

I lie awake at night wondering what my life would have been like if, as a child, instead of mashed peaches or softened bananas my mother had puréed a burrito or frappéd an enchilada. I'll never know.

Author's note: Now I'm having a pang of guilt. Truth is, I am happy about when I was born. If I had come into this world on any other day, I might not have met my wonderful wife, had such a great son, or been blessed with such a fulfilling career. Do you think I'm so stupid that I didn't realize that?

I wasn't born yesterday, ya know.

54

THE SPORTING LIFE

When the Wolfsies got back from our spring break in San Diego, man, were we exhausted.

I never realized how incredibly tiring it is to spend the day out in the blazing sun, experiencing what happens to the human body when the limits of endurance are tested. It's a good thing that the Wolfsies have stayed in peak condition or a trip like this would not have been possible.

It all began that first Saturday morning when my 18-year-old son—adventuresome daredevil that he is—suggested surfing. My wife and I are both in our 50s, but we still love a good challenge. We drove down to the shore and parked the car. We coated each other with sunscreen and spent the entire rest of the morning watching the surfers. It couldn't have been more exciting, but after a few hours the old muscles started to ache, and I knew that as good a shape as I am in, sitting that long in the hot sun is tough on the body. You have to know your limits.

My wife was not satisfied. "How about parasailing tomorrow?" she bubbled. My wife is six years younger than I am, so I understood her youthful exuberance. "Sure, why not?" I said, and the next morning we made our way toward the cliffs for another exciting adventure. I soon learned that this sport is far harder than it looks, requiring upper body strength as well as perfect manual dexterity. After about two hours I had had enough. I mean, how much of this can you watch without actually considering trying it yourself? I wasn't taking any chances.

That night at the hotel, we nursed our sore bottoms, but we were pleased by what we had accomplished that day—happy that we had made a choice to grab life by the lapels and really go for it.

The next morning we headed for a nearby mountaintop. Fortified with a good breakfast and possessing a real earnestness to experience this trip to its fullest, we tried hang gliding.

This is a difficult sport, requiring strong neck and back muscles because you must watch people ascend several hundred feet into the air and take flight above the treetops. We watched for over two hours. Perspiration soaked through our clothing and the sun wreaked havoc with our skin and eyes.

But the Wolfsies are not wimps. We wanted to pack in all the extreme sport we could.

The fourth day in San Diego should have been a day of rest and relaxation, but we knew that at some point we would look back and regret taking it easy. The hotel clerk told us about a shop downtown where people of all ages rented Harleys for a day and traveled Route 1, wind in their hair, discovering the rugged coastline. It sounded like a great idea. Sure enough, we got there just in time to see a young man about Brett's age and his grandfather (about my age) jumping on their Hogs and taking off. We stayed the entire day and watched the variety of people who were partaking in this activity. Remember, we didn't come to San Diego to just lounge at the hotel pool.

For our final day in San Diego my son suggested going to the world famous San Diego Zoo. It seemed placid compared to our other endeavors, but we went anyway. I enjoyed seeing the animals, but I did feel bad about their plight. They spent most of the day looking aimlessly through their enclosures, unchallenged by life as they would be in the wild.

After the exciting week we had in San Diego, I kind of felt sorry for them.

55

SURF TIL YOU DROP

I decided to do something last year for the first time in the history of my 25-year marriage. I guess I was going through a kind of (late) mid-life crisis and I needed a little novelty in my life. I knew that what I planned to do would create a lot of remorse, but I also hoped that under the circumstances my wife would understand.

I had also heard that unless you are very careful, you could end up with a pretty bad virus. That was not something I wanted to bring into our home.

Nevertheless, last year, I did all my shopping online.

I have felt very guilty about this. It's just not the same. Part of the value of each gift is the time and trouble you invested in buying it. That paisley scarf I got Mary Ellen last year would have seemed like a rather uninspired gesture had it not been accompanied by a dashing tale of mammoth traffic jams, throngs of hostile shoppers at the mall, and an untold string of rude salespeople. Of all the gifts I got Mary Ellen last year, she says the scarf was her favorite story.

The other problem with online shopping is that I usually buy clothes for my wife, but I have no way of knowing her size. In previous years I could at least ogle the saleswoman at Macy's and compare her body to my wife's body. (I'm able to explain this in print, but if I had used that same terminology at the store, they'd have slapped the cuffs on me.)

When you buy online, there is no salesperson to eyeball. Instead, you have something called a "virtual dressing room." I select a blouse and then the computer digitally applies it to the image of a woman who is supposed to be about my wife's size. Well, if my wife were two and a half inches tall this would be pretty darn helpful.

The result is that last week I had to rummage through Mary Ellen's closet and peek at the labels to see her size. Incredibly, my wife is a small in most things, a medium in others, and even a large once in a while. This kind of freaked me out and reminded me of an *X-Files* episode when some guy discovers that his wife is really an alien and can change into three different women. I sometimes feel that way about Mary Ellen after she's had two glasses of Merlot.

Regardless of whether I shop in person or online, I'm sure to mess up another Christmas. A couple of years ago my wife casually mentioned that it would be fun at bedtime to get into her pajamas and slip under the covers with a laptop computer. I thought I was pretty good at hints, but she just hated the pajamas I got her. Go figure.

Then just last year, prior to our 25th wedding anniversary, she kept walking around the house humming "I Love Paris in the Springtime." Well, it was pretty obvious what she was hinting for.

And yet when I surprised her with the sheet music with the lyrics, she seemed pretty disappointed.

Well, I think I better get back to my shopping. I hope we have a power failure or the computer starts to smoke. I'll never find the perfect gift for Mary Ellen, but she can always use a good story.

56

SURVEY SAYS...

Americans love surveys, but I can't imagine why. You show me any survey that gets front-page coverage and the results will always reveal that Americans are too fat, too dumb, or too immoral. There are surveys, for example, that tell us what percentage of men beat their wives. But how many bring roses home for no particular reason other than to say "I love you"? We'll never know.

Ever wonder how many adolescents are having premarital sex? There have been scores of studies. But how many teenagers wear clean underwear to school every day? No research has been done. We might be pleasantly surprised.

Americans are sleep starved. They did this survey by calling 10,000 people and asking them if they were getting a good night's sleep. They were

behind schedule in the research, so they had to make most of the calls around 11:45 p.m.

But that's just another example of what I'm talking about. All the results of these surveys are negative news. According to the research, for example, 50 percent of Americans can't get a good night's sleep. So where's the positive data? How many people are happy with their pillows? What percentage of people attribute success at work to their down comforter? How many Americans wake up bright and cheery due to the proper functioning of their electric blanket? No, this information is never revealed. We don't care about the good stuff that happens to people. Everything is bad, bad, bad.

Here was some more alarming news they discovered: Forty-five percent of Americans are addicted to sleeping pills. Almost 35 percent of Americans are high on Starbucks. The other 65 percent fall asleep on the way to Starbucks.

Americans apparently know more about *The Simpsons* than they do the First Amendment, or so says a new study by the McCormick Tribune Freedom Museum, a museum I never even heard of because I was too busy watching stupid stuff on TV.

Just how poorly educated are today's school kids? Researchers wanted to know, so they asked seventh-graders to name the five freedoms guaranteed by the First Amendment. When I was a young, you were considered a true American and potential Harvard material if you could name six dwarfs. If you could name all seven, some people questioned whether college was even necessary.

I remember years ago when I taught 11th grade geography, a study was published saying that only one in five high school sophomores could find the Soviet Union on a map. I got out a map the other day to see if I could still find this huge landmass after 25 years. I swear it's not there any more. If you've seen it, please let me know.

Another item in the research was that more people could name the three *American Idol* judges than could name three Supreme Court Justices.

That's the only good news I could find in the survey.

THANKS FOR THE MEMORIES

I tend to simmer about things a little longer than I should. For example, I'm still a little irritated they took *Alf* off the air after only three seasons. You don't get over something like that in just a couple of years.

Last year, I wrote about my New Year's Eve experience. I felt ripped off and decided I'd never go out on that particular night again. I was annoyed that despite what would be a $300 dinner bill, my waiter would not let me substitute the lobster bisque for an endive salad.

I got several letters from friends (mostly mine) telling me what a brilliant idea that was, not going out on New Year's Eve. I also received several letters from other friends (mostly my wife's) to remind me that I am a cheap, party-pooper, stick-in-the-mud. I appreciated every one of those letters (except the ones from my wife's friends).

To prove to me how much fun we would miss by avoiding this annual event, my wife suggested we reminisce about what we had done in previous years. Mary Ellen wanted to relive our past New Year's Eves with the hope of further rekindling that spark of passion. I yearned to do the same thing, but I wanted to know if we could do all that for about 200 bucks less.

We began with New Year's Eve 1978. We both had been invited to the same party. It's where we first laid eyes on each other. She thought this seemed like a good way to make her point.

"Think of it, Dick. That was one of the most glorious evenings of our lives. Good food, wonderful people, great conversation. And I met the most wonderful guy in the world. Do you know what I am trying to tell you?

"I sure do. For the price of a cheap bottle of Merlot, I had the time of my life."

But there were other New Year's Eves. A few back in New York.

"Do you remember New Year's Eve 1979, Dick?"

"I remember it well, Mary Ellen. We took your sister to dinner."

"I don't have a sister. Wasn't that *your* sister?"

"My memory's fuzzy. Do you remember '88?"

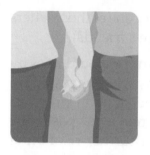

"Of course, Dick. That was the year we walked hand-in-hand in Central Park while the snow fell gently on our faces."

"Wow, that doesn't even sound remotely familiar."

"Oops, sorry. That was Rick in '78, not Dick in '88."

"I do remember 1987, Mary Ellen. That was my favorite of all. It was just a beautiful evening. The stars were out. I guess I just curled up and dozed off. You weren't angry, were you?"

"No, but the Times Square policeman was a little ticked off."

"Why can't they do that dropping-the-ball thing about 9:45? Where are the Baby Boomer lobbyists when we need them?"

The bottom line here is that I don't want to go out on New Year's Eve, but my wife does. Because of the kind of guy I am, I did agree to compromise. Next New Year's Eve my wife gets to go anywhere she wants and spend whatever she wants, but she's going to give me her lobster bisque.

CHANGE IS INEVITABLE

I've had it. It's over. I will never stoop (or reach) to that level again. Oh, I know I have said this kind of thing before. I swore I'd give up golf (and that lasted for three days during a rainy period); I promised to end my addiction to Mike's Hard Lemonade (I drink it after golf now); and I once pledged to forever be patient and understanding with my 18-year-old son who didn't do a darn thing around the house, forgot to mow the lawn, had a filthy room, wore raggedy sweat pants, and needed to shave and…

But this time I mean it. I will never buy anything from a vending machine again. Ever.

When I was kid, one particular "vending machine" had a good gimmick. In New York City there was a restaurant called The Automat. Inside was a wall that reminded you of the inside of a post office, covered with hundreds of compartments with shiny glass doors. Put in your coins, slide the door open, and reveal fresh apple pie, creamed spinach, Salisbury steak, meat loaf, or roast chicken.

Behind those little dispensaries was a mammoth kitchen. If you negotiated your gaze just right and peered behind the glass cubicles, you'd see dozens of bustling men and women in starched white uniforms sliding the cherry cobbler into the oven or basting the huge birds that would be roasted and made into turkey a la king.

The doors never got stuck, but if, on occasion, your favorite vegetable was not in its slot, you simply vocalized, in a very polite New York way, through the culinary porthole: OUT OF CREAMED SPINACH. Before you knew it, a friendly hand appeared and placed the succulent side dish on a real china plate within your hungry grasp.

Of course, I still offer my opinion to coin-op machines. Recently, in the WISH-TV dining facility (a room with four vending machines and a fridge with several two-year-old remnants of moo shoo pork), I lost my composure. I started screaming and punching one of the machines. Then I kicked it so hard that six Post-it Notes requesting refunds fluttered to the floor.

First, the Yodels didn't drop into the tray. Yodels, I have found, have a mind of their own. But, hey, I'm a flexible guy. Okay, no Yodels; I pressed Twinkies. Nope. Okay, how about BBQ potato chips? Still nothing. I pressed Dinty Moore Beef

Stew. Zip. How about a bagel and cream cheese? Nada.

Finally…celery and carrot sticks tumbled into the receptacle. Yeah, that's really what I wanted, anyway.

Last year in the United States, 14 people were killed by vending devices. When I first read this, I assumed it was the mayo in the tuna fish sandwiches, or maybe bad chicken salad, but apparently it was the machine falling on people who had lost their temper and began shaking the behemoth. They wanted Yodels and couldn't get them. I feel their pain.

Last week, I put 50 cents in a machine for a cup of coffee. I pressed extra cream, extra sugar, and extra strong. The piping hot coffee came bubbling out exactly as I had programmed it. Amazing. The fresh aroma of java wafted into my nose, but the precious liquid swirled down the drain hole. There was no cup.

Ain't technology great? Now they drink it for you, too.

WAIT A SECOND

In 2005 my good buddies over at the Naval Observatory decided to add a second to the end of that year. I just hope you are not getting this message too late. I'd feel terrible if you squandered the extra time.

This is what happens when really smart people have a little too much time on their hands. Your typical good old boys will short-sheet a bed or put Saran Wrap over the toilet bowl, but you put a bunch of Ph.D.'s in a room with 10 minutes left until lunch and you get what I call intellectual mischief. Egghead practical jokes, like exploding calculators and squirting laser pointers, were becoming old hat, so they came up with a legitimate scientific conundrum to drive us all crazy.

The rotation of the earth is slowing down and there was concern that if the scientists didn't make the necessary adjustment, the earth would be out of sync with the average person's watch. I already keep my watch set ahead 10 minutes to prevent me from being late, so I didn't lose much sleep when I heard the year was going to be a second longer.

Apparently, the scientists felt that if they didn't fine tune the time every decade or so, in about two hundred thousand years, we'd be having Christmas in May, which I always felt was a pretty good idea anyway because then you could buy all your Christmas gifts when the stores weren't nearly as crowded. And the weather was nicer.

This extra second was especially troubling to the people of Indiana who were already a bit on edge about Daylight Saving Time. You know as well as I do that in the spring when we had to adjust the clocks, there were countless Hoosiers who had not heard about the legislative change to DST. These are the same people who were shocked to learn that Governor Robert Orr is no longer in power. Or that Birch Bayh's son, Evan, went into politics.

In fact, decades from now TV stations will still be interviewing Hoosiers who can't figure out why six months of the year they are always late for work. Or would it be early for work? Whatever.

It was a good idea to tack that extra second on at the end of the year. At one second to midnight on New Year's Eve, most people out partying wouldn't know if you stuck in another week at the end of December.

So what did you do with that extra second? You probably think that nothing useful could have come from the additional time. I read somewhere that the last time they inserted an extra second was New Year's Eve 1978. I was at a friend's house for a party that night, and I noticed an attractive redhead across the room. Just a whisker before the clock struck midnight, I winked at her.

We've now been married 27 years.

60

WORD PERFECT

During my son's high school years, I lectured him constantly about spending too much time playing video games. I didn't make any progress. Maybe I should have waited until he took his headset off.

I remember telling him what a waste of time video games are and how little you benefit intellectually. Plus, the activity provides absolutely no exercise.

I would have lectured him more extensively, but the golf course near me had gotten new electric carts, so getting in 36 holes a day left little time for anything else.

My real concern was that my son would become addicted. Addiction is a scary thing. I should know. I have one.

Not to golf.

Not to nicotine.

Not to prescription drugs.

Not to Mike's Hard Lemonade.

I am addicted to SCRABBLE.

I don't mean the board game that is up in your hall closet wedged between your winter galoshes and the Monopoly game. And I don't mean the Scrabble game that you flung in your basement crawl space because you're missing a J and a V.

I'm addicted to the Scrabble that I downloaded on my computer. Oh, it's the same concept, only instead of playing your etymologically challenged brother or your linguistically deficient neighbor, you are playing Noah Webster and someone I assume is his obsessive-compulsive sister, Merriam.

Good luck.

In this computer game, you can control the level of difficulty, but with a degree in English, I'll be darned if I'll compete as a Novice or Beginner. Instead, I check off Expert, at which point the computer runs a program that has beaten all but 200 Scrabble players in America. They don't give me any names, so I'm wondering who these people are and if they also have wives and children who would like them to come up from the basement every once in a while and take a shower.

Every time I play, I realize I'm in over my head. Just before writing this column, I was trounced by the computer. Here were some of the words that beat me:

PROMIAL

ZOOTIER

HEWABLE

ZLOTE

SCHALENE

I have never heard of these words. Even my spell-check had a hissy fit. No such words, it told me by underlining them all in red. But, apparently, these 200 people use words like this as part of their everyday speech. This is just a guess, but these wordophiles must all live together in a commune, the perfect place for people who know the names of all 4,000 varieties of tree fungus, use them in conversation, and can spell them.

The reason computer Scrabble is so addictive is that every time I make a word that's worth more than 30 points, a nerdy little figure pops up on the screen and seduces me with adulation: GREAT JOB! EXCELLENT MOVE! I'm a sucker for this because I've only heard GREAT JOB maybe six times during my 25+ years of marriage. I can't remember ever hearing EXCELLENT MOVE! And I'm even counting our honeymoon.

My son is growing more and more concerned about my obsession. So much so, in fact, that he promised me the other day that if I gave up SCRABBLE, he'd give up video games.

"Just say the word, Dad," he told me. "Just say the word and video games are history."

The question is: What is the word? And how many points will I get?

61

YELLOW JOURNALISM

I walked out of Sam's Club the other day pushing my shopping cart laden with soft drinks, jockey shorts, a snow tire, and a year's supply of salsa. I was in a pretty good mood because I had managed to snarf down 14 of those tiny quiches without being fingered as a "repeat sampler."

The nice lady offering the hot treats did ask if I wanted to actually buy a box of the quiche, but I'm kind of a health nut, and they just had way much too much saturated fat.

I went through the checkout and when I got to the exit, the employee at the door asked me for my receipt. He stared at the slip of paper for a solid 20 seconds and then tried to assess my body language. At first I felt a bit embarrassed, like I had egg on my face, but it was probably just the quiche. They can throw you in jail for larceny, but not gluttony.

He never actually looked in my cart, just at the receipt and me, which I think is considered facial profiling. This has just *got* to be illegal. I think if this happened to Donald Rumsfeld, he'd switch to shopping at Costco at the drop of a hat.

As the stress was mounting, he took out his yellow highlighter and deftly clicked off the top with one hand, raising my hopes that I would soon receive that sought-after stripe that squiggles down the receipt and shows that you have truly arrived. Actually, it shows that you have truly left. Whatever.

Okay, so what's that stripe for? No one really checks your cart. You could have murdered the lady behind the lunch counter for disrespecting pizza, stuffed her on the bottom rung of the cart next to a 12-pack of Coors Light, and you'd still proudly make your way to the parking lot with a yellow stripe on that receipt.

Everyone gets a stripe: shoplifters, kleptomaniacs, pilferers, little kids with DVDs in their cargo pants. But still, I think the precautionary measures at Sam's Club are far better than at our nation's airports. I was in Washington, DC, one weekend and had to deal with security at Dulles Airport. I was searched by a professional frisker and then patted down by people who have made patting a new art form. I handed the agents my ticket, showed them two identification forms, took off my Rockports, and spread my legs.

And they call *that* security?

"Why don't you guys put a yellow stripe down my ticket with a highlighter?" I asked.

"Why would we do that, Sir?" asked the security agent.

"So you'll know."

"Know what?"

"Look, I don't know what you'll know, but I'll tell you this: There hasn't been a single recorded hijacking at a Midwest Sam's Club. Not one."

The agent didn't think that was very funny. And I know now that any form of comedy is frowned upon at the airport. I was told that I was the only person all day who was asked to completely undress for security purposes. I was kind of proud of that.

There's more than one way to earn your stripes.

62

ASTRONOMICAL STUPIDITY

I'm sure you have heard that Pluto is no longer considered a planet. You have to wonder why so much time was spent debating such an issue.

Is it a civil union or a gay marriage?

You're for it or you're against it. Who cares what you call it?

Some astronomers are calling Pluto nothing but an ice ball, which would be insulting to Plutonians, if there were any, resulting in a call to their version of the American Civil Liberties Union, charging some kind of interplanetary discrimination.

Quite frankly, I'm not really as bent out of shape about this as most people. The *World Book Encyclopedia* held up publication pending a final decision on Pluto's status.

This is the same book that went ahead and published its last edition before they knew if Brad Pitt and Jennifer Aniston were going to split and before anyone had actually seen Tom Cruise's baby to confirm it really was a baby and not just some little ice ball—like Tom. (Who, by the way, has just been demoted from movie star.)

Part of the emotional issue here is that a lot of folks grew up memorizing the planets using a mnemonic aid to remember the order of the spheres, and now that device doesn't work. So, they're afraid they'll end up on *Who Wants to Be a Millionaire* with no lifelines left and they won't be able to remember the eighth planet.

It's pretty obvious that My Very Excellent Mother Just Served Us Nutritious Pizza has to go. So, I've come up with this: Mortimer Virtually Exhumed Mary's Jingoistic Selfish Ubiquitous Nanny.

I just hope students appreciate all I've done to make today's astronomy easier. I'm always on the lookout for a way to help the younger generation.

By the way, I don't think most kids care any more about Pluto's downgrading than I do.

I mentioned this galactic change to a precocious 9-year-old who lives next door.

"Liam, did you know that Pluto was demoted?"

"You mean he's no longer a dog?"

So why was Pluto demoted? Apparently, in order to be an honest-to-goodness planet you have to be round, dense, and be in your own orbit.

My roommate at George Washington University in 1967 pretty much fit those criteria. I don't think Parker was a real planet, but maybe it's not too late. And if they did make him a planet, they could still keep that stupid original mnemonic device. P, Pluto, Parker…. See?

Hey, if you're going to start reclassifying things based on these new criteria, White Castle sliders would no longer be hamburgers. Do I have to go through this again? Not round enough, not dense enough, not big enough. They may be delish, but hamburgers, they are not.

End of story.

63

THAT'S THE TICKET

Do we discriminate against the elderly? I used to think so until I read about an 80-year-old man who was fumbling through his drawers (which is a funny image) and found a $1 parking ticket that he had gotten 60 years ago and forgot to pay.

Henry was apparently a man with an eye for a little publicity. He knew that someday he'd be 80 (with any kind of luck), and that if he conveniently misplaced the summons, he could pay it 60 years later when a buck was chicken feed, and he could maybe pick up a little positive press for seniors at the same time.

So why does this story about Henry irk me so much? Let me reexamine this case in light of a similar event in my own life.

I also forgot to pay a parking fine recently. It was a legitimate oversight. I, too, misplaced the ticket.

Actually, I put the ticket in my back pocket, went home, threw the pants in the Maytag, added a capful of detergent, and set the dial to "Heavy Soil." That's the last I remember seeing it. After that it was washed completely from my mind.

One month later, the BMV sent me a note saying that my fine had been doubled due to failure to pay. But I had just read this story about Henry and it started to bug me, so I made a quick call.

"Hello, is this traffic court? Just curious, have you heard about Henry, the guy who didn't pay his parking ticket for 60 years?"

"Yes, of course. What a heartwarming, uplifting, touching story about the inner goodness of human beings. We have his photo up on our court bulletin board as a lesson to all. He is so adorable. Who is this, anyway?"

"My name is Dick Wolfsie and I ..."

"Yes. Mr. Wolfsie. We have your photo up, too. Disgraceful, contemptible, horrendous."

"Look, I don't get it. This clown doesn't pay his ticket for six decades and he's a hero. I skip four weeks, and they double my fine?"

"Well, there's been some kind of mistake. We usually triple it after a month."

"How about after a year?"

"We'd probably revoke your license or garnishee your paycheck."

"How many years would I have to go before my failure to pay goes from horrendous to heart-warming?"

"How old are you, Mr. Wolfsie?"

"Almost 60."

"I'm afraid you don't have enough time left for heartwarming. I'd get your caboose in here or forget about driving to work."

I was thinking about this incident the other day. You see, about 30 years ago, I did something a bit dishonest, one of the few such transgressions in my life, and I have regretted it ever since. In order to get my first teaching job in New York, I told a little fib about my college record. Knowing they were looking for a social studies teacher, not an English teacher, I claimed to be a history major.

As a result of Henry's story, I have decided to head to my hometown and fess up to this wrongdoing when I am 80 years old. That's still 20 years from now.

Right now, you probably think I am a no-good despicable liar. But wait. In 2026 when I confess to the Board of Education, you're going to think I'm downright adorable.

WASHING MY HANDS OF IT

The newest trend in America is disinfecting. Everybody is doing it.

Coworkers, bosses, friends, neighbors.

Singles are sloshing their computer keys in sanitizer every morning at the office so they don't pick up any unwanted germs.

Then they meet someone cute on MySpace.com, and two hours later they're making out with a perfect stranger. Am I missing something here?

It's hard to go anywhere nowadays where people are not washing their hands or watching other people washing their hands, just to be sure they are washing correctly.

There are always instructions in the news on the correct way to perform this rather perfunctory process. I'm pretty embarrassed to say that I've been doing it wrong for nearly 60 years.

Of course, I've also discovered recently that I've been brushing my teeth incorrectly, waxing my car improperly, and dangerously compromising my eardrums with Q-tips.

It's amazing I've made it this far and still have a nice set of choppers and pretty good hearing.

My wife and I took a cruise where the waiters squirted a liquid into our hands just as we sat down for dinner. We were told this would prevent the transmission of disease.

We bought some of this same lotion for our next trip, to New York, figuring if there were any place waiting for a disease to be transmitted, it's New York.

But at the airport, security confiscated the bottle because they were afraid we might use it to make an explosive.

I think there needs to be a little more cooperation between the food police and the airport police.

When I was a kid, my mother made me wash my hands before meals.

I asked her why I had to do that since we often used utensils during family dining and hardly ever touched the food directly, except maybe the mashed potatoes.

My mother was easily intimidated by a solid intellectual challenge to her rules, so after that I never washed my hands before dinner again. What's really interesting is that, despite my unhygienic behavior, I never got sick or missed a day of school.

And talking about school, I never washed my hands before lunch there, either. But looking back I think the utensils could have used a quick rinse.

I read some astonishing findings by one scientist who couldn't get a grant to study the effect of Mountain Dew on rats, so he came up with this other harebrained notion.

Now it's all over the front page of your local paper, which by the way, according to this Dr. Gerba, is dirtier than the arm rest on your easy chair, but not as disgusting as your can opener, and is almost pristine compared to your shoe horn.

Dr. Gerba tells us that you would be better off, germ-wise, eating your lunch off a toilet seat than chatting on an office phone, an image that I have been having a heck of a time getting rid of when I eat an egg salad sandwich.

Dr. Gerba also advises against talking on your cell phone in a coffee shop—not that cell phones are a haven for germs, but he finds it especially annoying to put up with other people's personal conversations after he had to spend an hour in the Starbucks restroom scraping toilet seats, searching for germs for his Petri dishes.

By the way, I just heard from a friend who's a producer in Los Angeles that George Clooney has been seen romancing Sharon Stone. This has nothing to do with this topic, but I just thought after all this talk of disinfectants, you could use a little dirt.

65

SPINACH SCARE

The spinach scare of 2006 brought back a lot of memories. As a youngster, I was a little frightened of spinach, as are most kids.

That Popeye the Sailor connection was pretty clever, but even in 1958 as an 11-year-old, I knew a contrived promotion when I saw one. Clearly some adult wanted his kid to eat more green stuff, so he created a character who wolfed down the tasteless veggie instead of scarfing down a Yodel or a Twinkie.

Using a cartoon to sell spinach didn't work for me. Even back then, effective advertising usually involved some kind of implicit guarantee that use of the product would attract the opposite sex. But for me, a full decade before women went from a vague attraction to an obsession, I knew that I was not in the market for anyone who looked like Olive Oyl.

Anyway, this whole spinach scare, which I am sure was engineered by some elementary school kid as a fifth-grade project on "How Bad Press Can Ruin a Business," made me think about what role fruits and vegetables played in my growing up. Below, a partial list of produce memories.

Carrots: In my house, you always ate carrots raw. I have no memory of my mother ever cooking them, except it seems to me that a few crept into her beef stew. Just for color.

My grandmother always stressed they were good for your eyes, and her proof was that you never saw dead rabbits on the road. Possum corpses, on the other hand, were strewn everywhere. "Possums hate carrots," my grandmother informed me.

I know now what a bunch of hooey that was, but darn, that was a pretty good piece of propaganda, don'tcha think? I still like carrots and have never been hit by a car.

Thanks, Grandma.

Cauliflower: I hated cauliflower. Totally tasteless. And it looked like somebody's brain. But my mother saw my distaste as some kind of a challenge to her cooking abilities, so she would drizzle browned butter over the top of the stuff. Well, you drizzle browned butter over a wine cork and I'll eat it.

Nowadays you don't see cauliflower being served alone much. It's usually part of a medley. Cauliflower is like a tuba: It works in concert, so to speak. Tubas and cauliflower seldom go it alone.

Cranberries: My father loved cranberries, so my mother put them in everything: soups, salads, whatever.

To me they were pretty sour and disgusting, but at least they didn't look like a sheep's cerebrum.

In 1959 there was a cranberry scare. Something about toxic chemicals. The result was that the cranberry business was almost destroyed. I remember feeling really bad for the people who made a living growing cranberries. Yeah, right.

Peas: We never had fresh peas at home. Just canned peas. Yuck. First of all, they looked like ammunition from my BB gun, and there was no way you could get them on your fork because they scattered all over the plate like buckshot when you tried to capture a few.

A spoon would work to accomplish the task of scooping up the peas, but such activity was frowned upon and considered uncouth. My mother knew we hated canned peas, so she always served them with mashed potatoes. This allowed us to embed the legumes in a convenient and tasty temporary holding area until we consumed them.

And, now, here's what I think of Brussels sprouts.

Did you say, "No thank you?"

You took the words right out of my mouth.

66

HUNK DRIVING

Over the years I have made fun of scientific researchers for their obsessive fascination with bizarre and meaningless statistics. These are people who, statistically speaking, are among the unhappiest people in the world. Studies show that 57 percent of statisticians are 49 percent unhappier than 75 percent of all other scientists.

Here are a few examples of what the number-crunchers came up with: redheads need 25 percent more Novocain in the dental chair; 67 percent of men prefer gas to charcoal grills; people with pets wake up 45 percent more often in the middle of the night.

And now, the most incredible statistic of all — one that can affect the very fabric of our lives. According to the University of Illinois, people who are fat use more gas per mile than people who are thin. While driving, that is. If no one were overweight, we could save a billion gallons of gas a year.

What an astonishing figure! And, apparently, it *is* your figure that contributes to this excessive waste of a precious natural resource.

This information is vital because it helps Americans understand the crisis we face in foreign oil. Seems to me that the real crisis is more in domestic oil: Canola, peanut, and corn, all of which can take a simple potato and turn it into a cholesterol catastrophe called a French fry.

I mean, haven't we made overweight people feel guilty enough over the years? How do you think a chubby guy in his Toyota Corolla feels when some skinny Ph.D. in a two-ton SUV pulls up next to him at the service station and tells him that being a little paunchy is threatening national security?

Imagine telling someone who enjoys a Big Mac, large fries, and a Coke for lunch that if he would just switch to a plain turkey sandwich, he could get an extra mile per gallon for every 10 pounds lost. This was the real motivation of Jared, The Subway Guy. I see Jared Fogel around town every once in a while. He always has a huge smile on his face. Not because he lost 200 pounds; not because girls now chase him; not because he's an international celebrity; not because he is finally in good health. None of that. The guy is happy because last year he saved $6.89 in gas.

One problem is that there is no motivation for the people dispensing gasoline to cooperate in

addressing this problem. I went into a station the other day and my Speedy Rewards card receipt showed that I was now eligible for a chocolate doughnut, a free latté, and an egg and cheese sandwich. What a scam. Did they mention that by eating this, I was really going to end up spending more for fuel? Where are the lawyers when you really need them?

By the way, have you noticed that skinny waifs are out and the newest trend in the fashion industry is to feature models who have packed on a few extra pounds?

Don't ever underestimate the power of Exxon.

PYRAMID SCHEME

Just when you think everything in the news is too depressing, you see a headline like this:

ARCHEOLOGISTS SMILING ABOUT DENTISTS' TOMBS

Normally, finding funny stuff to write about is like pulling teeth. In this case, it *is* pulling teeth.

Tomb robbers broke into an Egyptian pyramid and found the remains of three Egyptian dentists. The robbers were arrested but their discovery has raised questions about the history of this medical subspecialty. That might make dentistry almost four millenniums old. Anthropologists said it wasn't hard to find a competent dentist in ancient Egypt. But a decent dermatologist? A good pulmonary man? Scarcer than hen's teeth.

Experts weren't sure they were dentists at first. In fact, there was some speculation they were lawyers because each was clad in expensive robes and jewels. Of course, they also could have been plumbers. What finally convinced the experts was the discovery of a huge 100-pound iron mallet nearby, which was apparently the Novocain of the day.

The dentists were lying right next to each other in the tomb, suggesting a group practice, the idea being that they could save a fair amount of overhead if they shared pyramid space.

The entry to the dentists' tombs was decorated with hieroglyphics that no one has translated yet. It is believed that these writings are probably an explanation of the dental health care plan 4000 years ago, and there is some hope that if it can be decoded, it might be a better arrangement than most of us have now.

By the way, painstaking translations showed one of the dentists' names was Ly Myr and the other was Kem Msw, which was probably Dr. Chuck Smith and Dr. Bruce Jones, but with all the cotton in your mouth, that's probably as close to saying it correctly as you were going to get. (I know that line makes absolutely no sense, but if I make myself laugh while writing, I usually keep the joke in).

According to the story, the mummified skulls of the male dentists were pretty decrepit looking (or was that decrypted looking?). But next to the dentists were the bodies of three females who died

with smiles on their faces, which just had to be the dental hygienists. I don't think things have changed that much.

The dental tomb was carbon dated at 4000 years old, but strangely they found some papyrus in the area that was dated 5000 years old, which they believe were magazines in the waiting room.

In those days, dentistry was not a profession without risk. One of the mummies had a spear in his belly, a pretty good indication that a dentist shouldn't say to a Pharaoh, "Don't worry, this won't hurt a bit."

68

My wife is a planner. She doesn't like surprises. This is not to say she is not a spontaneous person. Why, at the drop of a hat, my wife would jump into a cab (that she had arranged a week beforehand), then board a plane (if she had reservations two months ahead of time to get super-saver tickets), and head for some last-minute destination (more like 4000 minutes, but minutes none the less).

Even the hotel would be a spur-of-the-moment decision, once she had researched every Internet site for the best possible deal in the solar system. Yes, that's how impulsive she is. I can barely keep up with her.

But that being said, I was still taken aback by a question she posed to me recently on our way to a movie—a movie she chose after careful analysis of all the reviews, along with an online purchase of tickets.

"Dick, do you want a surprise party for your 60th birthday?"

"Excuse me?"

"Well, before I waste a lot of time finding a place to have a party, rounding up a few of your friends, and spending a lot on food, I just want to be sure you really want a surprise party. Hypothetically, of course."

"I know this is really narrow-minded and ungrateful of me, but isn't a surprise party supposed to be…you know…what's the word I'm looking for?"

"Well, how soon we forget. Do you remember what you said when I threw a surprise party for your 50th?"

"I seem to recall saying, 'Oh, you shouldn't have.'"

"That's exactly right—and I'm not going to make that mistake again."

"Okay, who would you invite to my surprise party? Hypothetically, of course."

"Well, to make things easier for me, you could just jot down some names on a piece of paper. And include some folks you wouldn't expect to come to your party. Maybe even a few people who aren't really that crazy about you. That way it really will be a surprise."

"I can't tell you how exciting this sounds. Is there anything else I shouldn't know?"

"Well, I don't want you to know exactly where the party might be, so come up with three places where you wouldn't expect people to jump out of nowhere, screaming SURPRISE!"

"Make it easy on yourself, Mary Ellen. Why not just have it at our house, and that way when I come home from work, everyone can just be hiding in the kitchen?"

"Well, how clever is that? They'd have to think you were pretty darn stupid to walk into your own home on the day of your 60th birthday with 15 cars parked on our cul de sac and not know something was going on."

"Okay, then, let's do it the day *after* my birthday."

"Hey, that's a great idea. I can't wait. This is going to be an even bigger surprise than you thought."

69

GIFT RAPPING

Men can't gift wrap presents. They don't know how. They don't want to learn. And it annoys them when they watch women do it. The few men who do know how to wrap gifts certainly won't admit to it, which is all part of the wrap, don't tell policy.

I am not one of those people who think men and women are genetically programmed for certain tasks in life. As I have reported in the past, Mary Ellen disagrees. She says that when we go out to eat, for example, my DNA dictates that I lead the two of us to the restaurant. Why? Because it was the prehistoric male who directed his family from territory to territory in search of a place to find sustenance. Of course, it was the woman who instructed the man exactly where to actually find the best provisions.

"So that means when we go out to eat, I have to drive, right?"

"Yes, Dick, but I pick the restaurant. You can't argue with biology."

"And tell me again why I get stuck unloading the dishwasher every night?"

"Loading is the key word, Dick. Loading the dishwasher, loading the camera, even putting a load of clothes in the washer satisfies an innate urge to attack. You can fight this impulse but you will never overcome it. Why not just quit complaining and start separating the laundry?"

But back to gift wrapping. Christmas morning everybody knows which gifts dad wrapped. In fact, it is a pretty universal notion that if the ends of the package are crumbled up like a big spit ball, it's a present from dear ol' Dad. If the package is wrapped in aluminum foil, it's a gift from dear ol' Dad. What if the package is turned over so as not to reveal the fact that not enough wrapping paper was taken from the roll to cover the box? Gee, could that be from Dad?

How much do men hate this chore? Have you ever seen males at a gift counter hoarding the items that come pre-wrapped? The average guy would buy his wife a gallon of anchovies if it came in a nice pre-wrapped box with a red bow on it.

Christmastime, I have generally tried to buy my wife big gifts. I don't mean big in the sense of expensive. I don't mean big in the sense of memorable. I mean BIG. Why BIG? Because when you give a big gift, it's okay not to wrap it. One year, I was thinking about buying my wife a terrycloth bathrobe. Have you ever tried to wrap one of those? Forget it. I bought her a washer-dryer combination, instead. Dragged it in the living room Christmas morning. SURPRISE!

Some gifts just require a big sheet thrown over them—like the year I got Mary Ellen a new exercise bike. Asking someone to wrap an exercise bike would be considered cruel and unusual punishment even in third-world countries where other forms of torture are acceptable.

This year, in order to make Christmas morning more visually appealing, Mary Ellen has agreed to wrap the presents *I* bought for *her*. Wait, she's calling me. I think her blindfold fell off.